~ *praise for* ~

Goddess Bless!

"Concise and easy to read. Sirona seems to have pulled together the essential elements for invoking the goddess in one's daily life."

—LADY SABRINA, AUTHOR OF *EXPLORING WICCA*

"There has never been, to my knowledge, such an in-depth, well-crafted book of Goddess blessings. Sirona has set a new standard."

—MICHAEL PETER LANGEVIN, AUTHOR OF *SECRETS OF THE ANCIENT INCAS* AND PUBLISHER OF *MAGICAL BLEND* AND *NATURAL BEAUTY AND HEALTH* MAGAZINES.

"Sirona Knight is a Goddess of words . . . words that move our spirit to take action."

—LAURIE CABOT, HIGH PRIESTESS, AUTHOR OF *LOVE MAGIC* AND *CELEBRATE THE EARTH*

Goddess Bless!

*Divine Affirmations, Prayers,
and Blessings*

Sirona Knight

Red Wheel
Boston, MA / York Beach, ME

First published in 2002 by
Red Wheel/Weiser, LLC
368 Congress Street
Boston, MA 02210
www.redwheelweiser.com

Cataloging-in-Publication Data available from the Library of Congress upon request.

ISBN: 1-59003-002-8

Typeset in Minion
Text design by Joyce C. Weston
Printed in Canada

TCP

08 07 06 05 04 03 02
7 6 5 4 3 2 1

For my mother, Betty
For my mother-in-law, Nancy
For my nana, Gina
For my grandma, Mabel
And for my grandmother, Vernal.
I love you all very much.
Goddess Bless each and every one of you.

☾

Contents

ONE: The Goddess   1

TWO: Affirmations, Prayers, and Blessings   14

THREE: Affirmations, Prayers, and Blessings
           for Daily Living   31

FOUR: Affirmations, Prayers, and Blessings
           for Love   53

FIVE: Affirmations, Prayers, and Blessings
           for Creativity   75

SIX: Affirmations, Prayers, and Blessings
           for Good Health and Vitality   94

SEVEN: Affirmations, Prayers, and Blessings
           for Abundance and Attaining Goals   120

EIGHT: Affirmations, Prayers, and Blessings
           for Peace and Harmony   140

NINE: Affirmations, Prayers, and Blessings
           for Greater Spiritual Awareness   155

           Goddesses Around the World   173

           Bibliography   182

~ CHAPTER ONE ~

The Goddess

Loving and gracious Goddess,
Let me know your perfect trust.
Where there is hatred, let me know love
Where there is doubt, let me know faith
Where there is sickness, let me know health
Where there is war, let me know peace
Where there is darkness, let me know light
So that I might go out in world as a candle
A reflection of your divine light
Twinkling like a star in the night sky
Waiting with expectation for the dawn.

☾

T HE Goddess represents a divine power as old as the Earth herself. As the universal "Mother," she is the source of all creation. Affirmations, prayers, and blessings offer ways to connect with and tap into her immense power.

The Goddess exists on many levels and affects your life in just about every way imaginable. She embodies the physical forces that regulate the basic flow of life. For instance, you don't plant a spring garden in the middle of winter. If you do, you are fighting the natural cycles of the Goddess, rather than embracing her power and help.

In her many forms and faces, the Goddess is divine energy that can help pattern behavior and influence emotions. As the primary force of creation, she has the power to help you create anything you can imagine. With her blessings, you can draw from her infinite power and wisdom and create a brighter, more loving life for yourself.

People call the Goddess by many names, but in essence, she represents a universal feminine power. She is all things to all people. Before the world and society turned toward patriarchy, she was everything that the paternal force of God later became to the early Christians. Now in the twenty-first century, the Goddess has reemerged and taken her place within the power of the divine.

The Mythology of the Goddess

Having evolved over thousands of years, the mythology of the Goddess offers you a cumulative energy. By gaining rapport with a certain Goddess, you open up a divine door that releases a powerful energy to inform and change you. Connecting with the Goddess power teaches you about yourself, both in terms of your priorities and abilities.

Myths and stories about the Goddess touch upon themes that are common to our mortal lives: birth, life, death, love, fear, and belief in the divine. There is a universal and timeless quality to mythology that continually inspires each generation who comes into contact with it.

As the symbol of creation embodying the eternal cycle of

birth, life, death, and rebirth, the Goddess is a fundamental and universal power. As the divine weaver in mythology, she weaves all things together into One. The Goddess acts as the supreme regulator and renewer of all life, controlling the seasons, the cycles of nature, and the movements of the sun, moon, and all celestial bodies.

The early Celts considered the Goddess to be the source of all creation. From her body and womb came all life. She offered the promise of wholeness because her knowledge came through the hearth and touched the spirit. Originally she was the sun, moon, Earth, stars, and all things. It was only later under Roman and Christian influences that cosmology was translated into paternal terms, in which the sun deity went from being a Goddess (female) to being a God (male).

In the process, society and spirituality moved toward more masculine attitudes about its relationship to the Earth and her feminine cycles. Rather than living in harmony with these cycles, people began trying to control and manipulate them. For example, living things such as trees, once revered and treasured as part of the Goddess, are now slaughtered and logged without regard to the future. Practices such as clearcutting and helicopter logging have left much of the land barren, scarred, and diseased.

The time for healing both the Earth and ourselves is right now! You can start today by using the affirmations, prayers, and blessings in this book. We can invite the feminine energy of the Goddess back into our hearts and spirits. Affirmations, prayers, and blessings are a step in this healing process, both personally and globally.

The Earth is a living entity that needs to be nurtured and respected. As we learn to nurture and respect the Earth and the Goddess, we will in turn learn to nurture and respect our selves, because spiritually we are extensions of the Earth and Goddess. It is time to become whole again and become one with the Goddess. As we do this, we will realize our full potential as human beings and spiritual beings of light.

Maid, Mother, and Crone

When I was young, I had dreams
Now that I am middle-aged, I have realities
When I become old, I will have memories
Each face connects to the others
And is divine and eternal
Just like the Goddess herself.

We all go through stages of life from the time we are born until the time we pass once again into Oneness, waiting to be reborn. As children, we find vitality and significance in every occurrence, no matter how trivial and mundane it may seem to others. As we progress into adulthood, we take on the unavoidable stresses of everyday life. When we enter old age, we have become at least somewhat wise to the ways of life. At this stage, we often have accumulated knowledge that would be nice to share with others so they don't have to go through the same trial and error as we did. In most traditional societies, the elders hold knowledge gathered throughout their life-times, and thus can teach the ancient knowledge passed down through each generation.

In terms of the Goddess, these stages of life are expressed as the three faces of the Goddess—maid, mother, and crone. An example of this is the Greek Goddess Hera, queen of Mt. Olympus and Goddess of women, whose three faces are the maid, Parthenos, the mother, Teleia, and the crone, Chera.

These stages of life not only happen on a physical level, but also on a perceptual level, where changing perceptions of yourself and your world impact and alter the very fabric of your life. The physical and perceptual levels greatly affect each other in the sense that as physical changes occur, such as those while growing older, the way you perceive the world and your life changes too.

Not only does the physical impact the perceptual, but the perceptual also in turn affects the physical. This is the idea behind energetic and psychic healing. By changing the ener-getic body, you change the physical body because of the con-nection between them. This is also the reasoning behind such ideas as positive thinking, healing with hypnosis, and psychol-ogy in general. Each one works off the idea that if you change how the mind perceives things, then you can change human behavior.

The ideas in this book are similar, in that the affirmations, prayers, and blessings are for changing your perception and as a result, your physical condition. I hope to introduce you to the concept of merging with and calling upon the powers of the Goddess in her many forms. This merging traditionally has been the basis for healing miracles and magical occurrences. Magic and miracles have always held an honored place within spirituality. After all, they are a sign that you have a sacred and positive connection to the divine. They represent divine blessing, love, guidance, and protection.

The Archetypal Faces of the Goddess

Mother Goddesses, such as the Celtic Anu, have many faces or aspects to them. The Mother Goddess unites all the other Gods and Goddesses into a divine family or pantheon, which traces its lineage back to her as the source of creation. By this virtue, every Goddess that stems from the Mother Goddess manifests one of her faces or aspects.

Beyond the three faces of maid, mother, and crone, Mother Goddesses have aspects that correspond to almost every facet of life, from childbirth and prosperity to love and creativity. Because of this diversity, you can select specific Goddesses that are most effective when doing particular kinds of affirmations, prayers, or blessings. For example, when doing a blessing for a safe childbirth, instead of using the Mother Goddess Danu, you could use one of her aspects, Coventina, who is a Goddess of childbirth. This modification gives a little extra directed power to your blessing.

Looking at the various faces of the Goddess gives you insight as to your own multifaceted personality, including how you relate to family, lovers, children, and coworkers, as well as how you deal with daily living, loving relationships, creativity, good health, prosperity, harmony, and greater spiritual awareness.

In this way, each face of the Goddess represents not only a divine energy, but also a human archetype. The Norse Goddess Frigga as a divine energy represents a deity who is a Goddess of love, wife of Odin, and queen of the Goddesses and Gods. As a human archetype, she represents the love that parents have for their child and the love that spouses have for one another. She is the face of the "Mother" and all that it entails, including a compassionate, nurturing energy that is the essence of the mother archetype in this culture. As such, the archetype becomes an energy that is given life and power in the whole of human consciousness. It can be tapped into and used by you as a source of empowering energy.

The Divine Feminine

As we move further into the twenty-first century, the divine feminine is making its presence known. After having survived the Dark Ages and persevering through the Industrial Revolution, the feminine polarity has once again begun to assert its influence. In the wake, Goddess spiritualities, such as Wicca and Celtic Druidism, have today become some of the fastest growing spiritual paths.

This is less a sexual revolution than a revolution of attitude and action. Instead of feeling superior to the Earth and cutting down all her trees, polluting her waters, and making her air so we can't breathe it, we must help our Mother in her time of need. Otherwise, she may not make it. If she doesn't make it, we won't make it either. If we kill our planet, Mother Earth, we kill ourselves, and all our future offspring.

Although the concept of the Goddess focuses on women and the feminine aspects of things, men can also benefit from working with their Goddess side, the feminine within. The bond between women and men is metaphysical, and thus part of it is rooted in the divine.

When men get in touch with the Goddess and their feminine side that stems from their mother, they don't become more like women. Instead, they become more in touch with their emotions. By learning to deal with their emotions, men can learn to better deal with their world. Instead of reacting explosively, they can learn to respond in different ways by blending the male element of fire and the female element of water into a combination that works.

For both women and men, the Goddess personifies a powerful inner force. It influences you in a great many ways. By gaining rapport with certain Goddesses, you open up a divine door, releasing a power that can ultimately teach you about yourself, both in terms of your priorities and abilities. This fresh insight can help you to set goals that will ultimately make you happy. You will discover what you want and that you really want it. But remember, an error in calculation results in an error in situation. In other words, if you have no idea what you want, then the divine does not know what to give you.

When you want something, it means you have an aspiration or goal. Your want activates desire, and suddenly you have an image somewhere located in your mind's eye that you can use as a guide. Things will begin to happen in what could be termed a "magical sense."

The keys to creating anything in your life are intention and expectation, desire and merging. Intention is what you want, and without it, there is nothing else. It is your foundation. Once you know what you want, make this idea real by using your senses—smelling it, touching it, feeling it, tasting it, seeing it, and being it. Expect it with every part of your being! The second step is to really want it, to strengthen your desire for it. The more you really crave something, the more you feel about it, the more likely it will come into your life. The last step is merging, which means that you become One with everything while communing with the Goddess.

It is important to gain rapport with the many Goddesses with whom you feel a special kinship. As mortals, we are all incarnations of her many faces. By building an energetic pipeline with certain Goddesses, you build a relationship of both give and take. This relationship is eternal, and with all puns intended, divine. By invoking this divine energy into your energetic pattern, you add a mystically powerful force that can help to change your life into something that you now only dream about. First you dream it. Then you create it, and finally, you experience it.

Merging with the Goddess is all about making your dreams come true, with a simple and ageless formula. When you dream, you develop goals and aspirations, and when you begin to construct ways for making these dreams real, the miraculous and magical occur. With a little help from the Goddess, you can make every day magical!

The Power of Goddess Affirmations, Prayers, and Blessings

When you tap into the power of the Goddess, you tap into divine energy. This energy has infinite potential to heal, create, and help you in your everyday life. Affirmations, prayers, and blessings provide a direct link to this divine potential.

Each Goddess has aspects that you can learn from and call upon, depending on your personal needs. In a sense, the Goddess is a divine representation of your humanness and a reminder that you are both human and divine. Working with the Goddess through affirmations, prayers, and blessings integrates your divine face with your humanness. One connects to the other. The divine is an important part of who you really are because it forms the spiritual center of your being. Without it, you are empty, a void waiting to be filled with everlasting light.

The Goddess embodies the Earth in all her splendor. We as human animals grow out from the Earth, and when we die we return to it. This connection between ourselves and the Earth was obvious to our early ancestors and formed their spiritual traditions. High Priestesses, priests, and shamans used this human-Earth connection to access the power of the Goddess by way of affirmations, prayers, and blessings.

Because the Goddess traditions evolved over time, they

contain a lot of ancient wisdom still applicable today, as the basic human condition has not changed, despite dramatic technological shifts. As mortals, we are still faced with birth, life, death, and rebirth as well as common issues of family, health, and love. A person of classical Greece would marvel at our technological advances, and she would think we had achieved Goddesshood by what we can do now—things people once thought were only done by the divine hand of the Goddesses and Gods, such as flying through the air in an airplane.

As far as our spiritual evolution is concerned, someone from classical Greece would not be amazed, because many of the spiritual and philosophical questions we talk about today are exactly the same as the ones Plato wrote about in the dialogues of Socrates. This is also why the plays of William Shakespeare, written in the seventeenth century, still have things to say to us within the context of our contemporary culture.

In this sense it is the human situation that has changed dramatically in the last millennium, whereas the human condition hasn't changed nearly so dramatically. Turning on an electric heater, powering up a computer, and driving a car sixty-five miles per hour down the freeway are situations that someone from 1000 A.D. would find incredible, bordering on miraculous. But in terms of the Goddess, these things are not miraculous, because the Goddess affects all aspects of life and is capable of many divine and magical things. Greek deities were constantly beaming themselves from Mt. Olympus down to Earth, not all that different from Captain Kirk or Picard beaming themselves to other planets or ships on episodes of *Star Trek.*

Goddess Bless

In the pages of this book, I sometimes refer to the Goddess as "Lady." The root of the word "lady" comes from the Old English word for "bread" or "kneader of bread," bread being one of the earliest foods produced from the Earth. The word "lady" is also described as being a woman who receives the devotion of a knight, lover, or disciple. Also the term "lady" is used as a courteous name that is interchangeable with woman or girl. Traditionally, "lady" meant a woman who was divinely connected to the Goddess or God on some level. This meaning is consistent with the way the word is used within "Goddess Bless!"

Even though this book is separated into various chapters and sections, often you will find much overlapping among the various sections. Being creative can bring you more abundance, peace, harmony, and good health in your life. In this sense, each chapter of this book is very closely related to every other chapter. This overlap can be helpful when you begin to finally learn to put everything together into One.

Besides the overlapping among chapters, there are also thematic links within chapters. Examples of this are abundance, where many of the Goddesses have a connection to cattle, an early sign of wealth, and divination. In addition, the Goddesses have a connection to time as being circular rather than linear. In this perception, the future is always there within your reach. All you need to do is access it. This can be done through affirmations, prayers, and blessings.

Goddesses of healing seem to have a connection to water, the force in life where everything flows in harmony. By connecting with the energy of the Goddess' energies, you learn to empower all the aspects of your life. Affirmations, prayers, and blessings are simple but effective ways to connect with and use these divine energies.

> *May the Divine Goddess guide me as I seek to heal and nurture the Earth and all of its creatures, to live in the midst of creation, and to love others as One, without regard to gender, politics, or spiritual tradition.*
>
> *—Based on the U.N. Environmental Sabbath for World Environment Day.*

☾

~ CHAPTER TWO ~

Affirmations, Prayers, and Blessings

*T*he power of affirmation, prayer, and blessing has been used for thousands of years in both spiritual and folk rites, by priestesses and priests, and by people trying to bring health, harmony, and happiness into their lives. In earlier times at the gigantic stone temples that dot the English countryside, high priestesses would call in the divine powers and blessings of the Goddess.

Many blessings and prayers have been passed down in oral traditions for generations before finally being written down. Often the old texts are wonderful resources for your own blessings, prayers, and affirmations. As with anything, their meanings change with time and use. Reinvented by each new generation, through time they have developed a mythic universality. An example is the following Goddess blessing, based on an old Irish prayer.

> *May the road rise up to meet you*
> *May the wind be always at your back*
> *May the sun shine warm on your face*
> *May the moon glow soft upon your door*

And the rain fall soft upon your fields
And until we meet again,
May the Goddess bless
And hold you in her loving arms.

Affirmations

Affirmations are statements of faith and belief that you repeat to yourself with emotional intensity for the purpose of attaining goals. They are useful and easy-to-use tools for creating a more joyful and abundant life without having to work harder.

To successfully do affirmations and achieve the results you want, you need to eliminate the negativity around you and sincerely believe you can manifest your destiny. You do this by reprogramming those thought patterns that are not serving you as well as they might be into positive, powerful affirmations. In this way, you can tap into the healing and creative power of the divine feminine.

Affirmations use positive thinking and dreams to align spirit, mind, and body with your true self, a step that will benefit every aspect of your life. The magic of affirmations is in the positive intentions and faith you put into them.

What you want is called "intention," and it is the guiding element in just about everything you do. In order to have a clear intention about something, you need first to know what you want. These desires are called your goals. Often your intentions are good, but because they are too general, it's difficult to define your specific goals.

In terms of the Goddess affirmations, prayers, and blessings contained in this book, you should be as specific about your intentions and goals as you can be. The more definitive you are, the more likely you will enjoy positive results.

Like most things in life, you have to work at what you want. The clearer your intention, the more likely you are to get what you want. Unlike control, which wants everything to work out in a set way, intention puts the suggestion out before the divine. After becoming One with the whole of the universe, the suggestion will filter back into the manifested world as an answer to your request.

Positive affirmation can take many forms and can relate to everything from waking up joyful in the morning, wanting good health, to bringing love, prosperity, and spiritual rapport into your life. There are no limitations as to how you can use affirmations to enrich your being.

You can gain rapport with the Goddess and access her divine power through affirmation. This helps transform your affirmation into reality, giving it an extra push toward success. In the affirmation, "Today and every day, with the help of the Goddess, I will bring greater spiritual abundance into my life. I am an irresistible magnet for all that the Goddess gives to me, and accept all her gifts gratefully," you are giving thanks for the help and insights the Goddess gives you.

Remember, divine powers don't always work on the same time schedule that you do. Because of this you might find yourself being visited by the Goddess and other divine spirits at odd times like three or four o'clock in the morning.

Prayers

When you bring divine energy into affirmations, they also take on certain aspects of prayer. Affirmations, prayers, and blessings all bring about change by first affecting the energetic body that emanates from the physical body. Many scientific studies show the correlation between the energetic and the physical, and that the energetic can heal physical illness and improve mental outlook.

Prayer is one of the most profound forms of human dialogue, regardless of the language. Individual or communal, private or public, prayer is powerful! The word "prayer" means to ask for something, and it is a major communication point between the mortal and divine worlds. Prayer is deeply relaxing and a form of meditation. It stems from a yearning from within—with empathy and caring—for a connection with the divine. Often times a crisis becomes an opportunity to grow on a spiritual level because through prayer, you often learn more about who you are and your connection with the divine.

Rupert Sheldrake, in his book, *A New Science of Life*, postulates that we all have fields that surround our bodies called morphogenic fields. These energy fields change when you pray, with collective prayer creating the largest field of all. In *Healing Words*, Larry Dossey has taken this idea further by saying that these fields of energy greatly increase when we are praying. He calls them "prayer fields."

Prayer fields are fields of energy that actually move out

from the body when you pray. Depending on intention and the depth of the merge with the Goddess, prayers can travel great distances, a phenomenon exemplified by the many cases of long-distance healing. When you pray with full faith that your prayer will help you, your blood pressure lowers, your anger vanishes, and you are more quickly able to tap into your potential for healing.

Our overall personal energy increases during prayer, which is the basis for connecting to the divine. Although we are all far from being Goddesses and Gods, we nonetheless reflect aspects of the divine. We are divine children with divine abilities that we can use to enrich our lives. We just need to get in touch with this power by using prayer.

We each have things we are good at and things we are not good at. Often through trial and error, we discover what these are, and we either accept them or not. Nothing is written in concrete, and life is always filled with surprises. Scientific and spiritual research continues, always teaching us something new. The absurdity of the past is the scientific tenant for today, and will most likely be on the garbage heap by tomorrow. Ideas that have universal appeal transcend the boundaries of time, while other ideas get lost along the way. Knowing the difference is one of the keys to making life better.

When discussing affirmations, prayers, and blessings, all of which ask something of the divine, it is important to differentiate between extrinsic belief which is thought about and done with the head, and intrinsic belief, which is felt through the heart or spirit. Making this transition from extrinsic to intrinsic belief is essential when doing affirmations, prayers, and blessings. Intrinsic belief has the ability to invite major personal growth in every area of life, including dramatic improvements in physical health, emotional well-being, and overall spiritual awareness.

Blessings

The word "bless" comes from the Old English words, "bletsian" and "blod," meaning blood, which derive from the blood kinship humans hold with the Earth—the Earth being the physical manifestation of the Goddess. When we bless, we hallow or consecrate by spiritual rite or word. To ask for a blessing invokes the divine for the care and protection of our personal life patterns. Our relationship with the Goddess is one of give-and-take, mirroring life itself.

A blessing is an approval or encouragement for your happiness or welfare. We ask for this approval and encouragement when we say, "Goddess Bless." Ask and accept divine blessing whenever you can, and it will make your life more enjoyable and divine.

Two concepts related to blessings are invocations and incantations. For purposes of this book, they are called blessings, too, although some of the blessings could be also termed invocations and incantations. All of the affirmations, prayers, and blessings have been created for the good of all and the harm of none.

Stemming from the Latin word "vocare," meaning, "to

call," to invoke means to call upon the divine, in this case the Goddess, for help or support. By enlisting divine help you give each aspect of your life new and added meaning. When you do an affirmation, prayer, or blessing, you are following a set formula for communing with the divine. You are calling upon the divine elements within and outside of yourself. The divine in this case is the Goddess, who in her many faces is a mirror to our many personalities. Connect these personalities in a way that works for you. When you get them flowing in harmony, suddenly things work more smoothly. It is important to move your mind from point A to point B. The closer the distance, the easier the task is to achieve.

We are all human aspects of the divine. In a lifetime, we live and die, but our divine spirit remains eternal. When we change our own patterns through affirmation, prayer, and blessing, we change the overall fabric or Oneness because we are all connected in a web of energy that unites the manifested and unmanifested. When we improve ourselves, we can help create a positive, joyful future for ourselves, our children, and for all of humankind.

How Affirmations, Prayers, and Blessings Work

Positive thinking works. It's a matter of having faith not only in the affirmation, prayer, and blessing, but also in who you are, without distorting that image into something that is not you. There are ways to empower yourself so you can go out and be in the world, and no matter what happens, you can come out of any situation with what you want and feeling good about yourself.

Affirmations, prayers, and blessings start out as a conscious process. Each time you get up in the morning and tell yourself you are a healthy, wonderful human being and that you are moving toward your goals, you are reinforcing the positive elements of the affirmation. The more you reinforce this feeling on a conscious level, then the more your subconscious begins to pick up on it. This ritual initiates change on a personal level. Suddenly you begin to have faith in yourself and in your skills. You realize that you have the ability to be the person you truly want to be. Any self-doubt that you harbored over the years begins to dissipate, replaced by a sense of personal power that previously you had only dreamed was possible.

Much of your self-doubt comes from your socialization, which begins at an early age with your culture, parents, siblings, and interactions with other people. Affirmations, prayers, and blessings can overcome this self-doubt and replace it with something positive. You are basically composting what doesn't work about your life, so it can be used to grow better and more healthy personal patterns.

Whenever I get nervous in a situation, I repeat the following phrase to gain a rapport with the Goddess: "I am the Goddess, the Goddess is me, we are One." Try chanting this over and over until you feel yourself entering an altered state. Then shout, "Ayea, Ayea, Ayea," feeling the energy in your body become whole and One with the energy of the Goddess. The three "Ayeas" are a way to release the energy.

Traditional shamans and high priestesses have long used altered states as a way of communing with the divine. In altered states, normal physical boundaries seem to melt away, leaving you open to Otherworldly and divine experiences. Your senses come alive in different and unusual ways. You become much more aware of all that is going on around you, including the energy and divine light of the Goddess that permeates everything.

How to Create Affirmations, Prayers, and Blessings

You can customize your affirmations, prayers, and blessings to fit your personal situation, making them even more powerful. After you do a few affirmations and begin to understand the simple formula, you will have fun adapting and creating your own.

Each affirmation, prayer, and blessing is directed toward a basic goal. You want a certain outcome as a result of repeating the affirming words. This is your expectation and intention. Sometimes the question, "what do you want?" seems unanswerable, but if you break it down into its different parts, suddenly the question won't seem quite so overwhelming. Take it a step at a time, and ask yourself, "What would I be doing in my life if time and money were not considerations?"

Affirmations, prayers, and blessings work best when they

address specific issues. When you begin creating your own affirmations, this is something to keep in mind. Work from the specific to the whole. Like double vision, you must always be looking not only at the present, but also how the present will affect the future. Your life patterns work on many levels simultaneously.

Modern psychology uses positive affirmations, prayers, and blessings as tools to help people change their mental patterns. Ancient mystery traditions used them as ways for communing with the divine Goddess, the Mother of all life. It is from her womb we are all born.

To create a simple affirmation, I begin with a basic phrase consisting of one or two lines. Keeping it short and to the point makes it easier to remember and makes repetition easy. A basic affirmation for healing is as follows:

> *Today and every day, I feel the healing power of the Goddess flowing through me.*

Once you have a basic affirmation to work from, you can then begin to tailor it to fit other situations and needs. If you are at period in your life where you need wisdom, you can change the affirmation to fit your situation.

> *Today and every day, I feel the divine wisdom of the Goddess filling my body, mind, and spirit.*

To give the affirmation more power, you can call upon a particular Goddess to help give you the wisdom you need. Keep repeating the lines until you begin to feel the power of that

Goddess entering into you. You may feel shivers on your skin, for example. You will feel a sense of wisdom in knowing that you are being helped to make the right choice. Imagine in your mind's eye the great Celtic Goddess Anu, whose main power was her motherly wisdom, as you repeat the following affirmation to yourself.

> *Today and every day, I feel the divine wisdom of the Great Mother Goddess Anu filling my body, mind, and spirit, and helping me to make the best choices possible.*

You can even add your name to personalize the wording even more. For example,

> *Today and every day, I, Sirona, feel the divine wisdom of the Great Mother Goddess Anu filling my body, mind, and spirit, and helping me to make the best choices possible.*

As with the old Irish blessing at the beginning of this chapter, another way of personalizing affirmations, prayers, and blessings is to adapt or rewrite one that you really love that fits the situation. Early Christians rewrote many pagan affirmations, prayers, and blessings, which took on a universal and archetypical nature over centuries of continual adaptation. The idea is to take something that works and make it better. Just change the wording so it's more personal and better suits your needs.

Successful Affirmations, Prayers, and Blessings

To make your affirmations, prayers, and blessings more successful, set up a sacred space for doing them, and imagining clearly exactly what you want to accomplish. By doing these two things, you give your affirmations, prayers, and blessings a place to be and a structure, which will provide better results.

To create a sacred space in your home, office, or garden for doing affirmations, prayers, and blessings, pick a place that is out of the way and private. It doesn't have to be anything elaborate, but just a space in your home or yard where you feel comfortable. Place an image of the Goddess or something that represents her in your space. This can be anything from a statue, a favorite rock, or if you're outside, a tree or plant that resonates with Goddess energy.

Besides something signifying the Goddess, sacred space objects that you have a kinship with work as well, such as a lucky coin for prosperity affirmations, prayers, and blessings, or the picture of a loved one when working on love. Other things you can bring into your sacred space include objects that signify the elements, such as incense for air, a candle for fire, a glass of juice, wine, or other liquid for water, and a potted plant in soil for earth. Beyond this, you can add most anything into your sacred space, such as scented oils or crystals and gemstones, that help you stay focused and directed when doing your affirmations, prayers, and blessings.

To make your affirmations, prayers, and blessings more successful, have a clear intention of what you want. By imagining what you want from the affirmation, prayer, or blessing, you give definite direction to where you are going with it. As you recite the line of an affirmation, prayer, or blessing, hold the image of what want in your mind: see it; feel it; sense it completely; be it! Once you step into the divine domain of the Goddess, you are summoning an energy that knows no bounds. You are releasing an eternal power that can wield incredible results!

When you adjourn to your sacred space, begin by reading the affirmation, prayer, or blessing out loud to yourself. When you do so you are engaging three senses: your eyes in reading, the sensation of your voice in your chest as you read, and your ears in hearing the words when you speak them aloud. As you read the affirmation, prayer, or blessing, feel its natural cadence. See it in your mind, feel it in your senses, and be it with your total self. When done in this way, affirmations, prayers, and blessings become a way for you to unleash your full potential.

The Power of Repetition

Verbal repetition has always been a part of spirituality. Many spiritual traditions, such as that of Buddhists and Druids, use repetition as a way for reaching a divine state. Reaching a divine state makes whatever you do afterward that much more powerful.

Keeping affirmations, prayers, and blessings short makes them easy to remember, repeat, and use wherever you go. Repetition creates an altered state, making you more receptive to the positive intention of the affirmation, prayer, or blessing.

An altered state can also make you more receptive to connecting with the energy of the Goddess. You can make affirmations, prayers, and blessings happen on your own, but when you ask for the divine help of the Goddess, you add infinite power to whatever you do. It is not a matter of control; it is a matter of cooperative intention. As I have stressed before, it important to have a clear idea of what you want.

The ancient technique of repeating the Goddesses' names for healing, guidance, and protection is at the heart of the practice of affirmation, prayer, and blessing. By using a particular Goddess's name, you invoke her power. By repeating her name, you create an altered state that builds a rapport with the Goddess. You enter into a divine state of being that is One with the Goddess.

In the case of longer affirmations, prayers, and blessings, the more you repeat the affirmation, the more impact it will have. The repetition at certain times of the day becomes a sort of tradition within your life. Building traditions is important when making patterns that you want to continue into the future.

Repetition is at the heart of the idea of patterns, which is what the Goddess is all about. The annual cycles of the Earth—spring, summer, autumn, and winter—are her many faces as she progresses through the year. In Celtic culture, it was the duty of the bard to remember and record through story and song the many blessings, invocations, and affirmations of the prevailing times. As they came down through the generations, these stories began to take on mythic qualities. This is the way of mythology. It is always being created and recreated.

The same is true of affirmations, prayers, and blessings. If one person says an affirmation, prayer, or blessing, it produces an energy that can change his or her life. If a billion people recite an affirmation, prayer, or blessing, its energy can change the very fabric of humanity. We could actually make human thought itself kinder and more compassionate and embrace love and peace as mainstays in our lives.

Timing and Practice

Affirmations, prayers, and blessings can be done during the day or at night. Just upon waking, just before going to sleep, and at set times periodically throughout the day are the best times to practice them. They work best when you incorporate them into your daily routine. Some of the best times for doing affirmations, prayers, and blessings are in the morning, before meals, when you are feeling stressed out or depleted of energy, and in the evening. At these times you'll find yourself more receptive to the positive effect that affirmations, prayers, and blessings can have on your overall psyche.

When you get up in the morning, your mind still lingers between the dream and waking worlds, making it more open to suggestion. By doing affirmations, prayers, and blessings before your mind has a chance to fully awaken, you have an open route into your subconscious.

Mornings are the time when most people begin their day, and as such, are a time of preparation and expectation. Morning affirmations, prayers, and blessings are best centered around the idea of revitalizing you and preparing for the day. Affirmations, prayers, and blessings that set daily goals and reaffirm your expectations for the day are excellent to do in the morning when the energy is fresh.

Before meals are a good times for affirmations, prayers, and blessings because most of us have a set time or pattern for meals on a daily basis. By incorporating these rituals into your mealtime, you give sustenance to your spirit, and at the same time, you give sustenance to your body. Also, before meals is excellent time to thank the Goddess for the food on your table and to ask for her blessings.

Often during the day you have times when the stress level goes way up or you suddenly feel very depleted of energy. Both of these are excellent times for doing affirmations, prayers, and blessings. You can do affirmations, prayers, and blessings that will calm and relax you, as well as invigorate and empower you, depending on what you need.

Evenings also offer an excellent time for doing affirmations, prayers, and blessings. Whereas mornings are about expectation, evenings are a time of reflection. Also evenings are usually a time of play and romance rather than work. Thus your evening affirmations, prayers, and blessings need to be more reflective but at the same time filled with love and merriment.

The eight-quarter and cross-quarter days called the Sabbats and the full moons are also good times for doing affirmations, prayers, and blessings. At these times the energy of the Goddess is greatest, so the power behind your affirmation, prayer, or blessing is stronger. Four of the Sabbats are the winter solstice, spring equinox, summer solstice, and autumnal equinox, with the other four being the half-way points between each of the first four. They are Imbolc, Beltane, Lughnassad, and Samhain.

Full moons are traditional times for doing healing rituals and invocations. During the year, there are either thirteen full or new moons. This means that most years, there are twelve full moons, but sometimes there is a thirteenth. The power of the moon exerts a lot of influence over the element of water and is closely tied to the monthly female cycle, making it also a time when the energy of the Goddess is most present. Besides healing affirmations, prayers, and blessings, full moons are also good for love and abundance. The following is an example of a full moon blessing.

> *Goddess, let me be blessed*
> *With your guiding light*
> *To light my way*
> *And lead me into a new day,*
> *One of love, abundance, and creativity*
> *By the Goddess, blessed be!*

☾

CHAPTER THREE

Affirmations, Prayers, and Blessings for Daily Living

I like to begin my day by doing an early morning affirmation to the Goddess. Do this affirmation as soon as you wake up, just when you are still drifting dreamily back and forth between the waking and sleeping states. Repeat these words:

> *Oh, Great Goddess, Mother of all things, I feel*
> *your divine light shine in every part of my being.*
> *Thank you, great Lady, for your divine presence*
> *in my life.*

Morning affirmations help you move out of a dream state and into a waking state, revitalizing your being so you can start the new day at your best. Bringing a Mother Goddess into your morning affirmations adds divine power to your affirmations.

Inanna, the Sumerian Mother Goddess, is an excellent choice to work with in morning affirmation. She brought civilization to humankind by persuading her father, Enki, God of wisdom, to give her the Tablets of Destiny and one hundred other magic implements of culture. Inanna loaded the boat of heaven with the treasures and sailed to her kingdom, Erech. Enki played seven tricks on Inanna to try and get back the treasures of wisdom, but in the end, the Great Mother Goddess was successful in bringing the wisdom of civilization and culture to people.

The following affirmations can be used when you wake up in the morning. Feel the wisdom and way of the mother Goddess as her energy revitalizes and awakens every aspect of your being.

> *Today and every day, I accept the divine wisdom*
> *and timing of the Great Mother Goddess. Her*
> *dance becomes my own. I align myself with the*
> *divine tempo of life as it unfurls moment by*
> *moment.*

> *Today, I recognize the Goddess within, and I*
> *allow her to move into and through all I do.*
> *Beginning right now, I bring her divine light*
> *everywhere that I am, shining it before me each*
> *and every moment.*

Ever since I was a little girl, I have always adapted the Lord's Prayer to a morning prayer I call "The Lady's Prayer." I felt more comfortable praying to the Lady, the Mother Earth. As an interesting sidelight, the plea for daily bread in the Lord's Prayer harkens to an earlier time when the Goddess was the giver of bread in her role as the grain mother and matron of bakers, mills, and ovens. She was the barley, grain, and corn mother. I say this prayer every morning.

THE LADY'S PRAYER

Our Mother who art all things,
Our Lady who art the moon, sun, and heavens,
Hallowed be thy name
By thy sovereignty of the sacred land,
Thy divine will be done
On Earth as it is in all realms
Give us this day our daily bread
Bless and guide us, Great Goddess
And protect us from all harm and evil
For thine is the power, beauty, and love
Forever, and a day. Ayea!

Use this morning blessing to begin your day, thankful for the blessings of the Goddess and for her rapport with you.

Goddess bless, for I am a reflection of you
Goddess bless, for I see myself in your many faces
Thank you, Lady, for your love and compassion
Thank you, Lady, for your beauty and wisdom.
Bless and thank you, Great Goddess! Blessed be!"

Affirmations, Prayers, and Blessings
Before Meals

Before meals is an excellent time for affirmations, prayers, and blessings. Use this one to bless your food before you eat. When you are with a group of people, substitute the "us" for "me" and the "we" for "I."

> *Goddess, bless this food you have given me*
> *Let it be filled with your divine energy*
> *So that I will be healthy*
> *And live a long and happy life.*
> *Goddess bless! Blessed be!*

The next affirmation is best done before breakfast. I call it "my goal for the day" affirmation because it focuses on the day at hand and can be changed daily, or you can keep the same one for as many days as it takes to reach your goal. The first part asks for the Goddess's help, and the second part states the goal. As an example I put the goal "more understanding of other people," but you can insert any goal you want, such as "Today, I see myself becoming more healthy in my eating habits," or "Today, I see myself becoming more loving toward my partner."

> *Goddess, help me attain my goal for the day.*
> *Today, I see and feel myself becoming more*
> *understanding of other people.*

Repeat the lines several times, while imagining and feeling yourself becoming more understanding of people.

In conjunction with this morning breakfast affirmation, do the following affirmation before dinner. They work together to reinforce your overall goal for the day.

> *Goddess, thank you for helping me attain my*
> *goal for the day. Today, I felt myself becoming*
> *more understanding of other people.*

The next affirmations can also be done before breakfast. They are designed to put you in a positive frame of mind for meeting the day, remembering that the power of the Goddess is with you no matter where you go.

> *With the help of the Goddess, my progress is*
> *constant and positive. Each day small miracles*
> *happen, and I become who I imagine myself to be.*

This morning affirmation can be used in conjunction with the previous one.

> *Every step I take is with the Goddess at my side.*
> *We are constantly moving forward. Together we*
> *are invincible.*

The Divine Power of the Mother Goddess

The Celtic Danu is the Great Mother Goddess of Ireland. The Irish families of Goddesses trace their lineage back to the Tuatha de Danann, who were literally the children of Danu (Anu). All the Goddesses are faces (aspects) of the Mother

Goddess. In this way, she is the persona where all things come together as One.

The first time I recognized this concept with all its underlying implications, it affirmed my own experience. Since I was a very young child, I have always seen light or auras around everything. This light connects everything together into one huge web of light.

The light, like the Mother Goddess, exemplifies the divine connection between all things in the universe, from the smallest atomic particle to the largest galaxy. Because of this divine connection, everything affects everything else, sometimes on many different levels, from the physical to the spiritual and energetic.

Affirmations, prayers, and blessings that emphasize this connectedness of everything are best done in the morning. You can also do them any time you feel unconnected from yourself, others, or the world. In this first morning prayer, feel yourself become the many faces of the Mother Goddess. In this case I use the Celtic Mother Goddess, Anu, but you can substitute any of the Mother Goddesses in her place in the affirmation.

> *Anu, great giver of life,*
> *I pray you,*
> *Let me see your many faces*
> *So that I might know the connection*
> *Between myself and all that is about me.*
> *I pray you,*
> *Let me see your face of Bridget*
> *So that I might know the light and fire in all.*

I pray you,
Let me see your face of Hertha
So that I might know the seed and potential in all.
I pray you,
Let me see your face of Anu
So that I might know the mother and nurturer in all.

In this next affirmation, you start with something small and keep building up larger and larger until you become one with the whole of the Goddess. You work with the concept of the Goddess in general, or use a specific Goddess to merge with when doing this affirming exercise. On the third "Ayea," feel your being diffuse and merge with the Goddess. Feel your energy expand until you are all things. Stay in this feeling of expandedness as long as you can, until at last you come back into your body.

After you are done, take a moment to remember what it felt like as the Goddess. If it feels like you are still carrying some of her energy with you, it is because you are. Carry it with you, and call upon it when you need it during the day.

I am the ink, the ink is me
I am the paper, the paper is me
I am the book, the book is me
I am the table, the table is me
I am the room, the room is me
I am the house, the house is me
I am the area I live in, the area I live in is me
I am the sky, the sky is me

I am the Earth, the Earth is me
I am the universe, the universe is me
I am the cosmos, the cosmos is me
I am the Goddess, the Goddess is me
There is no separation between us
Blessed Oneness—Ayea, Ayea, Ayea.

Any time you are feeling alienated from the world or from others, affirmations, blessings, and prayers can help you feel connected and centered again. They can help give your life more fullness and meaning. As you say the words in the following blessing, imagine being connected to the cosmos with strands of white light into a giant, bright web of energy. Repeat the blessing several times and each time, imagine yourself becoming more connected with everything in your world; more connected to yourself, your loved ones, your career, and your spirituality.

Today, I see how everything is connected
In an infinite web of light.
I now understand how I connect to everything
And how everything connects to me.
Blessed be the everlasting light of the Goddess,
May she weave a web of loving light
Blessed be the eternal love of the Goddess,
Goddess bless! Blessed be!

To enhance the affirming power of the words, take three deep breaths before you speak. Breathe in to the count of three, hold your inhaled breath in for three counts, and then exhale to the count of three. Then take a deep breath and complete an in-and-out breath before you say each line. Finish by taking three deep breaths, in the same manner as you did before, in and out to the count of three. Then repeat the blessing. Do this for about fifteen minutes. In this way, the blessing becomes a simple but effective affirming meditation.

Attaining Your Goals with the Harvest Goddess

Demeter is the Greek Goddess of the harvest, and her story corresponds to the seasons. In spring, she brings birth. In the summer, she brings growth. In autumn, she brings the harvest, and in the winter, she brings the cold, and nothing grows. In mythology, Demeter's daughter, Persephone, is taken from her to the Underworld, so in the winter, her heart turns cold while she weeps for the loss of her daughter. Then in the spring, her daughter returns, and all life is reborn again in Demeter's joy and happiness.

The following affirmations, prayers, and blessings acknowledge the Goddess of the harvest and her role in the food we eat, as well as in the patterns we set forth in our lives. Every goal is like a seed that is planted and allowed to grow and flourish before being harvested. After the harvest, you collect the seeds for the planting of the next pattern. In this way, life is a continual movement in a cycle that involves birth, life, death, and rebirth. Optimally, we learn from each cycle, moving the whole process forward. Otherwise, we repeat the same patterns over and over again, usually the patterns of our parents, which make us act out personalities not our own.

Demeter symbolizes both the Earth and all the edible plants that come from the Earth. Every time you eat a fruit or vegetable, you are eating something from the Goddess. It is her body that provides all life its sustenance. The next affirmations are about sowing, growing, and benefiting from the patterns and goals that you set for yourself. When you are happy, and your loved ones are around you, patterns come to fruition much more quickly and easily. Like Demeter, we flourish when our loved ones are around us.

Feel your connection to the Goddess and the food you are about to eat as you repeat the following two affirmations.

> *Oh Goddess of the harvest,*
> *I thank you for this meal*
> *Each bite I take*
> *Connects me to you.*

> *Earth Goddess,*
> *You are mother to us all*
> *Eating your fruits and vegetables*
> *Revitalizes my entire body*
> *Becoming One with your ever-animate spirit*
> *Revitalizes my entire being.*

Doing affirmations and prayers in the morning before breakfast is a powerful practice, because in the morning energy is at its most pure. Both prayers and affirmations are excellent tools for planting physical, mental, and spiritual seeds that you want to grow and see flourish in your life. By calling in the harvest

Goddess into the next prayer, you add divine energy to help
you to achieve your goals.

> *Bountiful Lady, thank you for your blessings*
> *Harvest Mother, thank you for your gifts*
> *Gracious Goddess, I ask for your guidance today*
> *Help me to flourish and attain my goals*
> *Blessed be the Goddess, Blessed be!*

Each morning, take a moment to imagine exactly how you
would like your life to be. Think about how you would like
your world to be without any personal or professional influences. Think about how you feel about what is going on
around you. Are you happy with where you live? Do you like
the work you are doing? Are you happy with where you find
yourself in life? Are you happy with your relationships? If you
could make some magical changes, what would they be? What
would you keep the same? What would you change?

Hold that positive image of the future in your mind for a
few moments. Imagine everything you ever wanted coming to
fruition, even your wildest dreams. As you do this, repeat the
words of the following affirmation, over and over (at least
eight times). Before beginning, take a couple of deep breaths
to center yourself.

> *Today and every day, I accept the overflowing*
> *abundance and love of the Harvest Goddess into my*
> *life. Her loving presence helps me attain remarkable*
> *success and prosperity. All of my dreams and goals*
> *are coming to fruition right now!*

In the following morning prayer, the harvest Goddess, Demeter, can help you attain your goals. As a Goddess of light, she provides insights into yourself and your connection to the divine.

> *Demeter, please help me attain my goals*
> *Great Lady, please help me*
> *Let every magical seed I plant*
> *Grow and come to fruition*
> *Let the harvest be sweet and abundant*
> *Great Lady, Demeter, please grant me this gift*
> *I ask this in our Lady's name.*
> *Blessed be! So shall it be!*

Personal Empowerment Every Day

When I was a junior in high school, I went to a meeting that a psychic was giving. After convincing one of my friends to come with me, we walked in and discovered that it cost more money than we had. Walking dejectedly back out to the parking lot, my friend and I were approached by two men, one of whom said he felt it was the economic considerations that were stopping us from attending.

He immediately looked at his friend, who smiled, and they escorted us inside and told the ladies at the table to let us in. My friend and I scampered in and sat in a seat up front. We were awed by the things the psychic did, things that we thought were not humanly possible. Being overly active and stressed out, the psychic said he calmed down by reciting the words, "I am a prince of peace on throne of tranquility." I liked the saying and later adapted it into a Goddess affirmation.

During the day when I begin to feel stressed out, I quietly recite this short affirmation to myself. Each time I repeat it, waves of energy pass through me, reducing and washing away my anxiety. At the same time, I come to feel calm and centered and filled with the power of the Goddess.

Repeat the following at least nine times. Each time you repeat a line, imagine your body becoming more relaxed. Feel yourself letting go of all the stress in this moment. Key in on the words "peace" and "tranquility," imagining your entire being moving into a state of calmness, from which you can now move forward in a positive way.

I am a Goddess of Peace
On a throne of a tranquility.

This next affirmation lets you know you are divine in every way, even when you're feeling down. When your spirit needs a boost, when you need to check back in with who you are and where you are going, recite these lines a few times. You will immediately notice an overall uplifting sensation.

I am a reflection of the Goddess
An aspect of the divine
I am She as She is me
And together we are One.

In Norse mythology, Voluspa is the most famous seer. Before the world began its present cycle, she foretold the future, including the doom of the Gods at Ragnarok. Her name is given to a poem that tells the story of the Norse Goddesses and Gods as well as Scandinavian wise women. The following prayer can help you connect with the divine wisdom of the Goddess Voluspa.

> *Voluspa, Goddess of sight and wisdom,*
> *Please let your powers flow through me*
> *Grant me the knowledge to know what I need*
> *Grant me the insight to know what I want*
> *Grant me the wisdom and strength to make it happen.*
> *Great Goddess, I pray you, make it so! Blessed be!*

When you have an important decision to make, you need as much divine help as you can get to make the best choice. The key is to see into the future as clearly as you can, imagining the consequences and effects of your decision. Like a new suit of clothes, try on these future effects to check to see if they work for you. If you don't like the way they feel, then make a different choice, and try it on.

This prayer can be used to tap into the powers of insight of the bright face of the Goddess to help you make the best possible choice.

> *Come, I pray you,*
> *Bright Goddess of wisdom,*
> *Bright Goddess of insight,*
> *I ask for your divine guidance*
> *Help me see into the future*
> *So that I will know the best choice to make.*

Come, I pray you,
Bright Goddess of light,
Help me see clearly.
Blessed be!

This next affirming blessing works along the same lines, but it emphasizes personal responsibility. As you begin reciting it, in your mind's eye, imagine yourself making the best decision and being happy with your choice.

I choose to take responsibility
For my decisions in life
Goddess, bless and help me in this task
So that I might make the best choices for me
Please help me be happy and satisfied with my
  decisions
Goddess, bless and guide me, today and every day.
  Blessed be!

Protecting Yourself and Loved Ones

The Persian deity Anahita is such a powerful Goddess that even the Great God Ahura Mazda worships her. Known as the "Golden Mother," Anahita drives through the world in a chariot drawn by four white horses. The horses signify the natural elemental forces of wind, rain, clouds, and hail. Tall and powerful, she is healer, mother, and protector of her people, whom she generously nurtures and fiercely defends.

Affirmations, prayers, and blessings can be used for

protection, both for yourself and your patterns in life. I don't think they are in any way a substitute for legal and necessary physical protection. Rather, you should combine intelligent actions and precautions against danger and harm with positive affirmations, prayers, and blessings.

When you feel the need for protection, use the following affirmations. While doing them, imagine a protective womb of white light surrounding and enveloping you. Initially it is easier to protect smaller spaces, but eventually you can make this womb as small or large as you would like through your intention.

This morning prayer can also be used for personal protection. Once again, feel the womb of white light surrounding you, protecting you from hostile, negative, and unwanted energies. If you like, imagine the power of the Great Goddess, Anahita, protecting and guiding you.

> *Great Goddess, I pray you*
> *Every day when I wake*
> *Protect and guide me*
> *May the Golden Mother stay by my side*
> *And let no harm descend upon me.*
> *Great Goddess, I pray you*
> *Blessed be, the Golden Mother!*

This simple prayer can be used for protecting your home and loved ones. As you repeat the following stanza, imagine the protective womb of white light expanding, surrounding not only yourself but also your home and loved ones.

Hear me, Great Goddess,
I pray you
Protect my home
Let no harm come
To me or my loved ones
Thank you, Great Lady!

This simple protection blessing can be used any time.

May the blessings of the Goddess
Protect, fill, and surround me
With divine light.
Now and forevermore.

Use this protective affirmation at night. Imagine the white light of the Goddess nurturing and protecting you.

Tonight and every night, I feel safe and protected
by the loving spirit of the Great Goddess. May she
cradle me in her divine arms and guide me
through the minutes of the night and day. I trust
the Lady to lead me in the right direction, down
the best possible path. May she bless and protect
me in my every step and in my dreams.

Evening Affirmations, Prayers, and Blessings

Bast is an Egyptian Goddess. In her earliest forms, she was a lion-Goddess of the setting sun, and later on, a cat carrying the sun, alluding to the life-giving and fruitful nature of the sun's rays. Besides being Goddess of the sunset, Bast was also the Goddess of pleasure, dancing, music, and joy. On those who invoke her into their sacred space, Bast bestows physical and mental health.

Morning affirmations, prayers, and blessings move you from a dream to a waking state and revitalize you as you get ready for the day. In your evening practice, you give thanks for any divine help. You evaluate your day with an eye toward tomorrow while relaxing and enjoying the evening. Try this simple evening blessing of thanks to let the Goddess know that you are thankful for her help, love, guidance, and gifts.

> *Goddess, bless and thank you for your divine help*
> *Thank you for all of the gifts you have given me today*
> *Thank you for your divine wisdom and protection*
> *Thank you for your divine love and understanding*
> *Thank you for accepting me into your divine being*
> *So that I might know myself and my divinity.*
> *Blessed be.*

Often a hectic day will leave you stressed out and scattered. This affirmation helps you put the pieces together. As you repeat the words, imagine beams of light gathering up and putting all your pieces back together again. I also suggest lighting a candle before doing this affirmation and using it as a focal point. This will add power to your efforts.

> *Goddess of wonder,*
> *Let your light fill my soul*

I am your candle
And with your love
I make my world whole again
Every moment of the day
I am your candle.

You can continue this affirmation by adding the following stanza. Repeat both verses until you feel reconnected and more centered.

I am the Goddess
And she is the light of my soul
She fills me with divine light
With her light, I become whole again.

Next, imagine what you want most in the world. Fix the image of it in your mind as you say this prayer.

In the rising moon
I see my reflections
One of who I am
And two of who I could be
Goddess of fertility,
Goddess of physical and mental health,
Make one and two the same
So that I might realize my divine dream.
(Now, state exactly what your dream is.)

The Phoenician Goddess Astarte, whose name means "womb" or "she of the womb," is the Goddess of fertility, maternity, war, and sexual activity. Because of her sexual nature, she is seen as the Goddess who rules over the planet Venus. As the morning star, she is warlike and wears a robe of flames while armed with a sword and two quivers of arrows. As the evening star, Astarte is the Goddess of desire, descending to the Underworld to reclaim her lost lover. This shows that while day is the time when people battle, the evening is for romance and relaxation.

I worked the night shift and got off at four in morning. As I drove home, which took me about an hour into the Sierra Nevada, I could see Venus as it rose in the east. I often felt as if the Goddess's light was guiding me home. Venus can be used as a powerful beacon of the Goddess, leading each of us where we want to go.

> *Venus, whose light blesses both the morning and*
> *evening skies*
> *Show me the path that leads me homeward*
> *A place where joy and happiness flow endlessly*
> *From the hearts and minds of everyone who lives there.*

As the evening star, the Goddess Venus can also be petitioned to bring more romance into your life.

> *Evening star, show me the face of my lover*
> *Bright and shining in your light*
> *Evening star, let me feel my lover's caress*
> *Flooding my being with desire.*

The following evening blessing is based on a traditional Chinook blessing. I often recite this to myself before going to bed.

I find it uplifting, and it sets the stage for dreaming pleasant
and divine dreams.

> *I respectfully call upon the animals, trees, and plants,*
> *Who have lived upon the Mother Earth.*
> *I call upon my ancestors, family, and friends*
> *Upon whose lives my life is built.*
> *With thanks and love and hope,*
> *I call upon you to teach me and show me the way.*
> *I call upon the dreamers who dream the dream*
>   *of living.*
> *I call upon all that I hold most holy.*
> *I call upon the presence and power*
> *Of the Great Mother Goddess,*
> *That great Lady of love, trust, and compassion.*
> *It is she who flows through all the cosmos,*
> *I call upon her and ask her to be One with me.*
> *Let her wisdom teach me and her light show*
>   *me the way*
> *To a way of life that is filled with love.*
> *May the Goddess bless, guide, and protect me.*

Do this next blessing just before you go to sleep. It blesses your
dreams so that they connect you to the divine spirit of the
Goddess.

> *Goodnight, sweet Lady,*
> *Goodnight, blessed dreamer,*
> *May my dreams be divine*

Blessed with images of the Goddess
Now and forevermore.

Finish your evening blessing by saying the following.

Goddess Bless all my dreams
Goddess Bless my spirit
Goddess Bless those I love
Goddess Bless those who love me
Goddess Bless, blessed be!

☾

CHAPTER FOUR

Affirmations, Prayers, and Blessings for Love

*T*he Greek Goddess Aphrodite stands out more than any other Goddess as the embodiment of love for those of us raised on a educational diet of Greek and Roman mythology. Formed from the foam of the sea, the long-haired Goddess Aphrodite rode the waves of the sea on a mussel shell. Landing on the Island of Cyprus, she shook from her hair the sea water, which immediately turned into beautiful pearls. She was attended by the lovely "Horae": Eunomia, Dice, and Irene, who are the Goddesses of the seasons and the order of nature.

Originally a Mother Goddess of the Eastern Mediterranean, Aphrodite was brought through stories by sailors to Greece, where she became the Goddess of love, beauty, and marriage. She also exhibits an influence on the fertility of plants and animals and is the symbol of feminine charm.

When a dispute occurred between Hera, Athena, and Aphrodite as to who should get the golden apple inscribed, "for the fairest," it was Aphrodite with her gift of love that the mortal Paris chose to receive the apple. This shows that love has always played a divine role in people's lives.

Ayea, Aphrodite,
Mighty Goddess of Love,
Fairest Lady of them all,
I ask for your blessings
For my lover and I tonight.

As a Mother and love Goddess who arises from the sea, Aphrodite embodies the power of water. The element of water figures predominantly in love because it signifies the moon and the feminine side of the divine. You can use quartz crystals to enhance the water/love connection when doing affirmations, prayers, and blessings by adding them to your sacred space, for example, on your altar, mantle, or bureau top. Water and quartz crystals have an affinity for each other because they share common elemental properties.

Throughout history, crystals and gemstones have been highly valued by spiritual leaders, healers, and scientists because of their high and exact rates of energy vibration. For example, quartz crystals can be used to amplify and balance the energy fields surrounding your body. They can also be used to increase the power of your affirmations, prayers, and blessings.

To activate your affirming words, hold a quartz crystal in your hands as you speak. Take a few deep breaths before you begin. Then imagine waves of divine love surging through and emanating out of the crystal with each word you speak.

You who are the Mother of All,
I feel your love cascade in waves all around me.
Every cell in my body resonates with love
As if awakening from a deep sleep.

You can also apply the energy of the love Goddess to arouse your passionate feelings toward life.

> *I am alive with the passion of life*
> *I am One with the Goddess of Love*
> *I am alive with the passion of life*
> *I am One with the Goddess of Love*
> *I am alive with the passion of life*
> *I am One with the Goddess of Love*
> *Ayea, Ayea, Ayea!*

Once Greek literature was influenced by Plato, Aphrodite became symbolic of spiritual love as opposed to mortal or everyday love. As Aphrodite's power grew among the people of the Mediterranean, there were great festivals held in her honor, called Aphrodisia. You can use the loving power of Aphrodite to delve into the deep, spiritual meanings of love.

> *Mother, did I tell you that I love you today? I love*
> *you. I am so thankful that you are always with*
> *me. Please help me create more loving*
> *relationships and help me know the deeper*
> *meaning of love. Blessed be!*

Love reflects many faces of humankind, from the love between a mother and a child, to the love between women and men, to the loving bond between a grandparent and grandchild. Use affirmations, prayers, and blessings to express these divine faces.

Your face reflects the love of the Goddess
Your eyes reflect the light of the Goddess
Your voice is the voice of the Goddess
You are a divine child of the Goddess
I love you, forever and a day.

I am a loving, caring, and passionate person.
I am worthy of love.

Dear Goddess, may I know love, love, and be lovable
I pray to you, Great Lady, divine source of compassion
Hold me in your arms so that I feel your loving light
May I awaken to the light of my own true nature
May my heart always be open to my grandchild
   (insert name)
And may we always walk together in beauty and
harmony.

Goddess, bless those I love and care about.
Please help guide and protect my loved ones
Now and forevermore. Blessed be!

Transforming the Past with the Goddess

Love isn't a battle or competition. It's a cooperative effort between two people bonded by divine love. The foundation of love must be trust rather than deception. Otherwise, the relationship eventually crumbles from the distrust and negativity.

In order to move forward, you must let go of past experi-

ences, particularly those painful relationships and past set-
backs. It's essential to improve upon what works as you let go
of what doesn't work. Accentuate the positive, while you eliminate the negative. When you begin doing this, you will find
that you are a lot happier.

The following prayer can be used to rid your body, mind,
and spirit of any feelings you may still have from painful relationships in the past.

> *Dear Goddess, help me, lovely Lady,*
> *To put love where there is hatred*
> *To put hope and faith where there is doubt*
> *To put joy where there is sorrow*
> *To put harmony where there is discord*
> *Please help me to heal my pain*
> *Help me learn the spirit of forgiveness*
> *Grant me your divine wisdom*
> *So that I can love and be loved again.*
> *I ask this in the Lady's name, so be it!*

This approach is both practical and empowering. After all, you
can bang your head against a wall for only so long before it
starts to hurt. Some things are worth fighting for in love and
some things are not. Ultimately, you must decide. The best
way to figure it out is to ask yourself how you really feel about
people and things. Once you do this, you begin to understand
the deeper meaning of love and what types of love work
within your life. You recognize those people whom you cherish and those who empower you. You begin to treat yourself

and those you love with greater respect, compassion, and kindness.

This next two-part affirmation uses the divine love of the Goddess to help you let go of your past hurts and replace them with feelings of love.

> *Today, I listen carefully to the loving voice of the*
> *Mother Goddess. I hear the divine gift of love and*
> *hope in her every word. Like a soothing melody,*
> *her loving voice calms and sustains me each and*
> *every day. As I listen to her, I feel all pain and*
> *sorrow being lifted from me. I feel my spirit being*
> *filled with love until love is all I feel.*

This next affirmation is also about releasing your past and making your present and future more loving. Being of a more reflective nature, it is best done every evening. As you speak the words, reflect upon your past with feelings of love.

> *Tonight and every night, I look through the eyes*
> *of the Goddess. I see the past with love. Knowing I*
> *am learning from my experiences, I bring the*
> *positive gifts of the past into the present.*

The Grace of the Goddess

Aphrodite's divine attendants are called the Graces. In Roman mythology they are known as the "Graciae," and in Greek mythology they are the "Charites." They are dancing goddesses who embody the grace of manner.

Always gentle and polite, these three Goddesses, together with Aphrodite, rule the realms of love. They are Thaleia, who brings abundance, Aglaia, who brings splendor and radiance, and Eurphrosyne, who brings joy and happiness.

The three Goddesses of grace represent the delight in living a creative life of art, dance, music, beauty, and love. Mythology indicates that the Graces are older than Aphrodite, and that they met her when she first arose from the sea. Metaphysically, the Graces embody grace, loveliness, and charm, with the myrtle, rose, and musical instruments being sacred to them.

Affirmations can be used to express the love of life and its many daily wonders. Life is an adventure of love that unfolds like the petals of a rose, transforming into a beauty that is boundless. Following the course of the three Graces, the next affirmations present the ideas of abundant, splendorous, and joyful love.

I am filled with the infinite and abundant love of the gracious Goddess. Her divine power pours like light through every facet of my being.

I feel the splendor of the Lady's grace and love in my every breath, every thought, and in every step I take. She surrounds me with the warm golden light with the brightness of a thousand suns.

I feel a joyfulness toward all things that comes from the loving grace of the Goddess. Each

morning when I awaken, she fills me with the joy
of love. Each evening when I dream, she fills me
with the joy of love.

Affirming Your Love

Affirmations, prayers, and blessings are the perfect way to
express how much you care for others and how much you love
yourself. While you are doing the next affirmation, try holding
a piece of rose quartz in your right hand as you speak the
words. Rose quartz exhibits natural qualities of nurturing love
and compassion.

> *Today and every day, I am one with the divine*
> *love of the Goddess. I am willing to do all I can to*
> *make a loving environment for those people I*
> *really care about, including myself.*

In a Celtic love story, the young maiden Grainne decides to
marry the much older Finn MacCumal, leader of the Fianna,
whose heroic exploits are legendary throughout Ireland. At the
feast held before the wedding, Grainne falls in love with one of
Finn's entourage, the young Diarmaid.

There are several explanations as to why she falls in love
with him, one story being that he has a magical love spot on his
forehead that makes any woman fall helplessly in love with him.
At first, Diarmaid rejects Grainne's advances, citing his allegiance to his leader, Finn. Then she bestows her magical power
over him, in the form of a magical oath or "geis," urging him to
take her away. Diarmaid consults his companions in the

Fianna, who tell him that his bond with Grainne, the "geis" known as a druid's oath, is stronger than his allegiance to Finn.

Upon discovering Grainne's trickery, Finn pursues the lovers throughout Ireland, almost catching them. Each time they escape with the help of Oenghus, God of love, who instructs them never to sleep two nights in the same place. After chasing them across most the countryside, Finn is eventually convinced to forgive the disloyalty of Diarmaid. Free at last, the lovers eat the fruit from the tree of immortality, transforming them and their love from mortal to divine.

In the tradition of Grainne and Diarmaid, you can use the power of affirmation and prayer to find your soulmate and form lasting spiritual bonds.

> *Great Goddess, please guide me in my quest for love*
> *I put my faith in your hands*
> *And my future in your divine wisdom*
> *I am a ship of love looking for friendly shores*
> *Lead me to lands I've never been before.*

To add more power to your affirming words, experiment by holding a thumb-sized or larger clear quartz crystal in your dominant power hand while speaking. As you speak the words, look deep into the crystal to see the image of your lover. If you feel you have already found your soulmate, use the affirmation to reaffirm your feelings and visualize your lover's face inside the crystal.

Before beginning, clear the crystal of any energies before and after using it by grasping the crystal in your power hand and seeing in your mind a clear mountain stream washing the crystal clean. Breathe this image into the stone. Or you can soak the crystal in sea salt and water for a few minutes, rinsing it clean in clear water for about a minute. For more information and techniques on clearing and using crystals for personal empowerment, please consult my *Pocket Guide to Crystals and Gemstones* (Crossing Press).

Begin the affirmation by staring deep into the latticework of the crystal. Merge and become one with the stone, while repeating the following words:

> *Goddess, let the waters of love flow through me*
> *Like a river running into the ocean*
> *Goddess, give me clarity so that I might see*
> *My divine lover's image in the crystal.*

If at first you don't see anything, repeat the affirmation while merging even deeper into the crystal. See the crystal, feel the crystal, and be the crystal. If you still don't see anything, try invoking the power of your favorite love Goddess, and alter the words of the affirmation accordingly.

> *Aphrodite, Goddess of Love,*
> *Let the waters of love flow through me*
> *Like a river running into the ocean.*
> *Aphrodite, Goddess of Love,*
> *Give me clarity so that I might see*
> *My divine lover's image in the crystal.*

If you still don't see you divine lover's face in the crystal, then try closing your eyes, and seeing your mate's face in your mind's eye. Either with the crystal or in your mind's eye, the image may be blurry to begin with, but as you keep repeating the affirmation, the image will become clearer and more defined.

Affirmations, prayers, and blessings can be used to bring more love into your life by helping you find a new primary relationship or by strengthening your current one. The pronoun "he" in the sixth line can be changed depending on the gender of your lover.

> *Golden Lady of the dawn,*
> *Help me to bring more love into my life*
> *In the form of a lover who will love me*
> *Unconditionally for who I am*
> *And whom I will love unconditionally*
> *For who he is.*
> *Golden Lady of the dawn,*
> *Fill my life to the brim*
> *With the abundance, splendor, and joy of love.*

Love is a bond that transcends lifetimes. As you speak the words of this "Wishing Well" Goddess blessing, feel your spirit connect to the spirit of your lover before ascending to a place of sublime love, a place where the light of the Goddess always shines brightly on you and your beloved.

> *Penny in the well*
> *Dreams come true*
> *Bless us, Great Goddess,*
> *Let my beloved and I*
> *Become one spirit.*

Penny in the well
Dreams come true
Bless us, Great Goddess,
Let my beloved and I
Know a higher love.
Penny in the well
Dreams come true
Bless us, Great Goddess,
Let my beloved and I
Always be together
Forever and a day.

The Three Faces of Love

Like the Goddess, the spirit of love has three faces: the maiden, mother, and crone. In its maiden face, love is fresh, alive, adventurous, and filled with wonder, much like the season of spring, when the annual cycle of life begins again.

As the mother, love is nurturing, mature, fertile, and protective, like a mother bear watching over her cubs.

As the crone, love is wise, healing, teaching, and guiding, much like an ancient oak tree, whose roots and branches stretch out every which way into the earth and heavens.

In its three faces, love becomes all things to all people, much like the Goddess herself. Many Goddesses of love embody these three faces in one form or another. For purposes of this book, I have selected the Goddesses Freya (maiden), Frigga (mother), and Sheila na Gig (crone). Affirmations for each face of love follow the description of the corresponding Goddess.

Love and the Maiden

Freya, whose name means "the lady," is the Norse Goddess of love. She rules over plant life, trees, animals of the forest, female sexuality, magic, and the love between women and men. As the Goddess of fertility and physical love, Freya is the one whom lovers call upon for assistance in love affairs.

The Goddess travels through the nine worlds of Norse mythology wearing a cloak of falcon feathers in a chariot pulled by either cats or bears. She is also the leader of the Valkyries, who are divine female riders in the sky that honor the bravest of the fallen warriors.

The following affirmations use the maiden face of love to empower your love life, helping you to make it more positive and satisfying. Rather than a physical state, the face and energetic power of the maiden is more of a mental state of being. Every time you fall in love again, even if it's continually with the same person, you experience the loving face of the maiden, without regard to your physical age. In this way, the maiden is always with you throughout your life.

This first affirmation is about being in love, when you have that feeling of floating somewhere between the earth and sky, where love takes on a magical quality that transcends everything else that you feel. Your heart flutters and pounds. You begin to sweat, and your spirit soars higher than it ever has before. In its essential state, the maiden face of love can

make it impossible to eat or can send you to places that connect you with the divine power of Goddess.

Everything looks brighter, sounds sweeter, feels finer, and
tastes and smells better when you are connected with the Goddess. Being in tune with the Goddess enhances and improves
every aspect of your life. You become One with the spirits of
the earth, air, fire, and water. You become One with she who is
the Mother Goddess of all things.

Try to remember the first time you fell in love. What were
the sensations? No matter how your life turns out and who you
become, the feeling of falling in love for the first time is something that everyone has in common. It's part of the common-
ality of being alive. The following affirmation expresses the joy
of that feeling.

> *I feel like a spring day*
> *Alive with the feelings of love*
> *I feel like a well pouring forth*
> *Energized, revitalized, renewed*
> *Alive with the feelings of love*
> *Music sounds better than it ever has before*
> *The fragrance of flowers is sweeter*
> *I'm alive like never before*
> *I'm flying through the air*
> *I'm walking on sunshine*
> *I'm dancing on water*
> *I am a part of the Earth*
> *She who is my mother*
> *I am star-born*

I am the shining moon
I am the maiden
I am the Goddess of love.

This next affirmation is designed for lovers to say to one another. It's all about the first time you saw your beloved and the timeless quality of your love.

The first time I saw you
You were the essence of love
I felt something lift me above the trees
You are my divine love
Someone I've known for lifetimes
Somewhere in time
I was you, and you were I
Drawn together through time
As One. Blessed be!

You can use affirming prayer to ask the Goddess for her blessing of love for you and your beloved. If your beloved is open to the idea, pray together.

Great Lady, bring the magic of love into our life
Please give my beloved and me your blessing
So that we might know your divine power
Great Goddess, please receive and guide us.

The love in relationships often rises and recedes like the tides of the ocean as they feel the energetic pull of the moon. In this next affirming prayer, you call upon the Goddess to fill your relationship with love.

It is love that I seek
As I call upon the Goddess
To aid my lover and I in our time of need
Great Mother, I pray you
Fill us full of your divine love
So that we may again become One.

When sharing a quiet moment alone, say these affirming words of love to your beloved. Then have your lover repeat them to you.

I love your eyes
And everything I see
I love your touch
And everything I feel
I love your smile
And everything above
I love your spirit
And the essence
Of who you are
To me you are a shining star.

Love and the Mother

Frigga in the Norse tradition is the Goddess who came before all the other Goddesses. Her mother was Fyorgyn, the Earth herself. Goddess of the sky and clouds and of married love, the tall and stately Frigga dresses either in the plumage of hawks and falcons or wears long white robes that can reflect the many hues of the sky.

Frigga spends most of her time weaving clouds of various colors or spinning the golden thread that is the raw material that the three Norns weave into the web of a person's fate. Personifying the Earth, Frigga has eleven handmaidens or will-doers, who go out into the world on her behalf, attending to the well-being of mortals. They smooth the paths of lovers, preside over married love, spread knowledge, and administer justice.

When you ask Frigga to help you with your affirmations, prayers, and blessings, you call upon the power of the Earth, mother to us all.

I am the Earth
She is me
The trees are my bones
The rivers are my blood
The air is my breath
And the Fire is my life
Together we live
First as two
Then as One,
I am the Earth
She is me
The rocks are my stability
The wind is my spirit
Passion is the fire
The ocean is my boundless love
Together we are One.

You can also give thanks to your mother, both in a physical and spiritual sense with this blessing.

> *Mother, you gave me the light of life*
> *It was your spirit who made me who I am*
> *Thank you and bless you*
> *May you always be with me*
> *Blessed be!*

You can also ask the divine mother to protect your child or children. As you recite the following verse, see a white protective light coming down from the sky and enveloping your children and filling them with the love of the Goddess.

> *Mother, please protect and guide my children*
> *Whatever they do and wherever they go*
> *Let them always know your divine light*
> *And may you be forever in their hearts.*
> *I ask this in the name of the Goddess.*
> *Thank you, Mother. So be it! Blessed be!*

Mothers are many things to many people. This next affirmation acknowledges the divine nature of motherhood. The mother of the family is most often the balancing force that keeps the peace. She is the cohesive power that holds a family together. Let this balancing and cohesive energy flow through you.

> *I love my divine mother for who she is*
> *Just as she loves me for who I am*
> *I release any pain I may have had with my mother*
> *in the past*

So that I can become One with the divine Mother,
I feel the Goddess Mother's nurturing spirit
As it flows through me
Balancing and connecting me to Oneness.

Love and the Crone

Sheila na gig, whose name means "hag" or "Sheila of the breasts," represents the crone face of love. A powerful Irish Goddess, she is depicted in pictures throughout Ireland as an old woman, grinning, with a bony face, large buttocks, and a full bosom. Her statues are found next to wells and springs, in gardens, and in other sacred places.

Sheila na gig is associated with the vulva or yoni, which is considered a holy symbol that represents the passageway of life and death as well as the entrance to or exit from the womb of the Earth Mother. As such, Sheila na gig is a Goddess of fertility, whose image in the past was seen on stones and carved on Irish doorways, where she was used either as a protection, blessing, or as invitation to the feminine mysteries.

Sheila na gig is also a Goddess of regeneration, who has a connection to the Otherworld, and because of this she has traditionally been used for harnessing feminine power or for revealing past and future lives.

On our planet Earth, trees are some of the oldest living entities. Find an old tree (an oak works well if you're near one), and put your hands on its trunk as you recite the following verse.

Ancient tree, long have you lived
Please impart your wisdom to me
So that I might know all of your wisdom
And together we might be One.

Ask for the wisdom of the crone in life, and in creating a lasting and loving relationship with your beloved.

Wise one, tell me what I need to know
To let the flame of love burn eternal
Let my lover come to me
With open arms and an open heart.

Ancient and shining one,
I can see forever in your eyes
Each point leads to another
Till the ancient wisdom of love is revealed
Love of life
Love of self
Love of Goddess
Love of everything
Love of the One
When all is revealed
They are all the same
The wisdom of crone
Resides within us all
And when I look within
I tap into this spirit,
Ancient, and all-knowing.

*In my elder years, I am the crone. I honor the
threefold Goddess within. I still laugh and can be
silly and play. I am still passionate and full of
lust. I continue to create beautiful things, and I
look forward to the smile of a new day as
something new and different than what was
yesterday.*

*I live in the present, rooted in the traditions of the
past, ever mindful of the patterns of the future.
Today and every day henceforth, I love and
cherish who I am in my many faces of maiden,
mother, and crone.*

Bringing More Passion into Your Life

The Babylonian Goddess Ishtar has a kinship to the Sumerian
Mother Goddess, Inanna. But unlike the timid Inanna, the
moon Goddess Ishtar is more akin to today's Powerpuff Girls
who are powerful, protective female cartoon characters on tel-
evision. When she went to the Underworld to retrieve her
lover Tammuz, she demanded entry at the gate of death,
threatening to smash it open and let the dead out if her
demand was not met.

Not only does Ishtar rule the moon, but like the Phoenician
Goddess Astarte, she rules the morning and evening stars, symbolic of the warlike and passionate energies of the feminine.

As the morning star, Ishtar's name is "Dilbah," and she
roams the morning sky, dressed in armor, while driving a

chariot drawn by seven lions. As the evening star, her name is "Zib," Goddess of desire and sighing, whose song is sweeter than honey and wine.

When the energies of the morning and evening stars combine into a Goddess of sensual sexuality, she has no comparisons among other Goddesses. Displaying two main aspects, the compassionate Mother Goddess and the lustful Goddess of sex and war, her rule over the fertility of the Earth is linked to her role as the Goddess of sexual passion, whose sacred animals are the lioness and the dove.

> *As the Goddess of the hunt and divine passion*
> *Many have compared me to the rose*
> *Whose intricate beauty and wildly enticing fragrance*
> *Is offset with the protective thorns that scar the hurtful*
> *I am a lover beyond compare*
> *During the day I am the huntress*
> *During the night I am the seductress*
> *I am the love, I am the passion*
> *I am the lioness of lust.*
>
> *My lover and I lay here covered by the lustful*
> *energy of the passionate Goddess of love. Here*
> *together, we are separate, yet divinely One.*
>
> *Tonight and every night, I am a lustful lioness*
> *and a loving dove.*
>
> *Each and every day, I feel the divine love of the*
> *Goddess. I am able to love my beloved and myself*
> *unconditionally.*

☾

CHAPTER FIVE

Affirmations, Prayers, and Blessings for Creativity

I will begin with the Muses.
For it is through the Muses
That there are singers upon the earth
And players upon the lyre,
Happy is she whom the Muses love
Sweet flows the speech from her lips.
—(adapted from the Homeric Hymn
to the Muses and Apollo)

*I*n ancient times as well as today, the Greek Muses embody the ultimate expression of creativity. These nine Goddesses are universal symbols of the creative force. Through them we can connect with the divine, kindle our ideas and dreams with Goddess energy, and keep the channel open for creative inspiration.

When asked about creative inspiration and where it comes from, many writers and musicians often refer to their muse. They talk about tapping into a feminine creative energy that comes and goes, a wellspring of ideas that communicates directly to them. The muse is most often spoken of as a divine gift to cherish but never control. To do so only stifles her inspiring gifts.

In modern western culture, the word "Muse" is the name of a rock and roll band as well as the title and subject of a delightful Albert Brooks movie. As you can see, the ancient Muses still light the creative fires of artists from many genres, from painters and poets to composers and authors.

The nine Muses were originally three nymphs who presided over poetry and the arts of music. One of the more accepted stories about how the Muses were created comes from a Greek myth. After the gods defeated the Titans in their epic battle, everyone requested that Zeus create divinities capable of putting together the celebration of the millennium. To accommodate them, Zeus bedded Mnemosyne, Goddess of memory, for nine consecutive nights, and as a result she birthed nine daughters who become the nine Muses, Goddesses of the creative arts.

From the Muses come all tales, songs, and inspired knowledge. Myths provide archetypes for both the way things are and the way things should be. The Muses tell myths to mortals. This is why bards, when telling a myth, began by saying, "Tell me, muse" or "Sing, Goddess." By doing so, the bard acknowledges the divine origin of the tale.

Plato called the gift of inspiration a poetical madness, a condition that must stem from the divine. "A third kind of possession and madness comes from the Muses. This takes hold upon a gentle and pure soul, arouses it and inspires it to songs and other poetry, and thus by adorning countless deeds of the ancients educates later generations. But he who without the divine madness comes to the doors of the Muses, confident that he will be a good poet by art, meets with no success, and the poetry of the sane man vanishes into nothingness before that of the inspired madmen" (Plato, Phaedrus 245a). Myths operate and exist by the power of memory and the Muses, on the golden thread that both separates and weaves everything together into a divine web of Oneness.

The Nine Muses and Their Creative Blessings

1. CALLIOPE

Her name means "beautiful voiced." The Muse of epic and heroic poetry, she is often depicted with a tablet and pencil. Calliope is the oldest of the Muses and often considered their leader. In one instance Zeus called upon her to mediate the quarrel between Aphrodite and Persephone about Adonis. Calliope settled the dispute by giving each Goddess equal time, while also giving Adonis some free time for himself.

Because she is the Muse of epic and heroic poetry, Calliope is a master at the art of putting words and rhetoric together in the best way. When she is the Muse that helps stir your creative fire, you can be assured that you are divinely inspired. Try this muse-inspired blessing in the morning.

Oh Fair One, Lady of poets,
Grant me your blessing
So my words shall be divine,
Grant me your blessing
Let my creations be inspired by you,
Here and now and forevermore.

2. CLIO

Her name means "fame giver." As the Muse of history, Clio is usually depicted with a laurel wreath on her head while holding a trumpet in one hand and a book or scroll in the other. She introduced the Phoenician alphabet in Greece. Clio is also the Muse who teases Aphrodite about her love of Adonis, provoking Aphrodite's wrath. In retribution, Aphrodite causes Clio to fall in love with Pierus, the king of Macedonia, by whom she is the mother of Hyacinthus.

As the Muse of "herstory," Clio is the perfect Goddess to invoke in your blessings when you need a sense of history about what you are doing. This history might include ancestral roots as well as writing and making history. History is being made all the time. To record history is to influence what is being reported. When you look into the past, you also see into the present and future, because time is not linear, especially divine time.

The following two blessings ask for the aid of the Muse Clio, to help in a current creative project that you are doing, and to help you through a turning point in your life.

> *Wise Muse of history,*
> *I ask for your blessing*
> *Let the creative project I am working on*
> *Withstand the test of time.*
>
> *Lady of wisdom, blow your trumpet*
> *Sound the call so all will know*
> *Today marks a turning point in my life*
> *Please bless and guide me, wise Great Goddess.*

3. MELPOMENE

She is the Muse of tragedies and songs of mourning. She is usually shown wearing or holding a tragic mask, the club of Hercules, and a wreath made of vine leaves. She is also the mother of the Sirens, whose beautiful voices mesmerize those who hear their sweet sound.

Invoke the Muse Melpomene in your blessings when you are either working on a creative project that is a drama with tragic overtones or when you are working out some personal tragedy in your life, either past or present.

> *Goddess, please help me through this period of life*
> *Grant me your loving strength and help me see the*
> *   light*
> *Even when things are confusing and tragic*
> *Help me to see beyond all of my sadness and pain*
> *To a time when everything is brighter*
> *And in creative harmony with the divine.*

4. EUTERPE

As the Muse of music and lyric poetry, she is the "joy giver" and "giver of pleasure." Called "she who makes herself loved," Euterpe is depicted with a flute and a crown of garlands made from flowers. Euterpe is also the inventor of the double flute.

When composing a song that involves writing lyrics, Euterpe can help you be divinely inspired. The following blessing is intended for this purpose.

> *Oh, giver of pleasure,*
> *Lady of flutes and flowers,*

Lovely and loving Muse of music,
Help me write a song today
Worthy of your inspiration
Please bless my song
With divine lyrics and music
Inspiring all who hear it.

5. ERATO

Called the "awakener of desire," Erato is the beautiful Muse of love poetry who also inspires erotic poetry. She is often depicted holding a lyre and wearing a crown of roses. She is also a Goddess of mimicry and pantomime. Traditionally a pantomime was a performance featuring a solo dancer and a narrative chorus.

The best time to invoke Erato's blessings is when you are writing a love or erotic poem, a love story, or doing love magic. You can also ask for her blessings and guidance, for instance, when you are working on a ballet or story told by dancers who use expressive body movements or facial gestures.

Lovely Muse, awakener of desire,
Please guide me as I create
Let me hear your loving words
Help me to express myself divinely
In a way, lovely Lady, that conveys,
Your blessings and inspiration.

6. TERPSICHORE

Known as the "lover of dancing," Terpsichore is the Muse of dancing and music, in particular the choral song. Because of this, Terpsichore has an association with singing. In addition she plays the flute and the kithara, a stringed instrument larger than a lyre.

Terpsichore is the ideal Muse to ask for blessings in all creative projects that involve singing, especially choral singing, songwriting, and dancing. She is the master of movement and dance and has a voice that can either light the world on fire or sound as sweet as the most melodic songbird.

> *Sweet lover of dancing and music,*
> *I call upon your strength and power*
> *Bless me, great Lady of song,*
> *Let me sing with the divine voice of the Goddess*
> *Let me dance with the divine grace of the Goddess*
> *May I be One with your creative essence*
> *May I be One with the essence of the Muse.*

7. URANIA

Her name means "heavenly," and she is the Muse of astronomy and cosmological poetry. She is often pictured with a globe and a compass. While the Muse Clio is associated with history and the past, Urania looks toward the future and to what the stars bring, as the star patterns symbolize the future. For Urania, time is circular rather than linear, and past, present, and future become one. After all, Urania and Clio are sisters, meaning in the end, it's all family, which is what Oneness is all about. We are all connected to everyone and everything else.

When you invoke the creative blessings of Urania into your life, you align yourself with the cosmological order governing all human activity. The basic battle is between the forces of chaos, which represent the breakdown of any kind of form and creative substance, and the forces of creativity, where everything is gifted with a life that is divine and dances the dance of time. Creativity, in this way, connects the past to the future.

> *Heavenly Muse, star Lady,*
> *Star light, star bright*
> *First star I see tonight*
> *Please bring me heavenly wisdom*
> *Bring me divine creativity*
> *Bless and guide me, star Goddess.*
> *Blessed be the heavenly light.*

8. THALIA

Her name means "to bloom." Thalia is the Muse of comedy, idyllic poetry, festivity, and humor, and she is often depicted wearing a comic mask, crowned with an ivy garland, and carrying a shepherd's staff. Thalia is honored at the European Feast of Fools on December 28th. This is a day to laugh out loud, throw a party, and do something that inspires you to blossom.

Asking the Muse Thalia to bless your creative projects helps them to bloom. Her power gives them a feeling of festiveness and mirth that is an important part of creativity. A feeling of playfulness often enhances creativity, not to mention day-to-day life. Seeing the humor in things can also help you keep your sanity when everyone around you is losing theirs.

Oh Muse of mirth and poetry,
Sweet and joyful bloom of the Goddess,
Please grant me your divine blessing
Let me see the humor in everything
May I always be in your infinite graces.

9. POLYHYMNIA

Her name means "many hymns," and she is the Muse of hymns, mimic art, and harmony. Polyhymnia is sometimes depicted as dressed in white, with a flower or pearl crown, her left hand holding a scepter.

Invoke Polyhymnia's divine blessings when your creative project is of a spiritual nature. Traditionally, hymns were songs of praise, usually to the divine. Polyhymnia is also the perfect Muse to help create more harmony in your personal and professional life.

Praise be to the Goddess
Who is all things to all people
Today I sing her song
So all will know of her greatness
She is the Earth
She is the wind
She is the Sun
She is the rain
May she bless me with her melody
And bring divine harmony
Into my life, now and forevermore.

The Divine Connection

When Mahisasura, the colossal buffalo monster, threatened to undo the world and send it back into chaos, all the Hindu deities came together and combined their powers into one supreme warrior. So the Hindu divinities poured out their energies as fires that rush together, assuming the shape of the Goddess Devi. Armed with the weapons of the gods and riding on a lion, Devi roped the monster Mahisasura, but the horrible beast escaped by shape-shifting into a lion. The Goddess Devi quickly beheaded the lion, but the monster again shape-shifted, first into a hero, then into an elephant. The Goddess finally defeated Mahisasura when he returned to his buffalo form, thus saving the world from the forces of chaos.

Because of her creation as "the Goddess," all Hindu forms of divinity can be reduced to Devi, and without her no "good" would have power or form, for she gives birth to all force and form. She is the Goddess who creates separation out of unity, and is the energy that continues to protect the world from chaos. In her light face, Devi is Gauri (the yellow), Parvati (the mountaineer), Uma (light), and Jaganmata (mother of the world).

When someone realizes that there is a mythic or divine quality to what she is doing, the insight triggers an inspiration that can only be termed divine. In terms of affirmations, prayers, and blessings, the more active and pronounced your efforts, the higher your level of success. The divine in this case is the hand that stirs the creative cauldron. This first blessing is

to the Goddess of all creation. Use it every morning to help
you awaken the divine light within and ignite your creativity.

> *Oh wondrous one,*
> *Giver of all form,*
> *Please bless and guide me*
> *Grant me your divine spark*
> *So I may light a thousand suns.*

The next two affirmations are reminders that the Goddess is
always with you, helping you to be more aware of your divine
connection with her and her many faces.

> *Today, I consciously remember to listen to the*
> *voice of the Goddess. Even in the midst of my*
> *daily activity, I know that the divine feminine is*
> *birthing herself through me, awakening my*
> *creativity and making all things anew. Blessed be*
> *the Lady!*

> *Today and every day, I am empowered by the*
> *Goddess of creation. I rejoice, knowing that I am*
> *connected, as One with the divine creativity of*
> *the Maid, Mother, and Crone. Thank you, Great*
> *Lady, for your daily blessings and inspiration.*

Creative Inspiration

Many a Goddess has inspired great works of art. Kindling the
creative fire is a specialty of the Celtic fire Goddess Bridget,

whose name means "bright one" or "exalted one." Down through the ages, Bridget's sacred fire was never allowed to go out. To do so would bring doom and destruction upon humankind.

Daughter of the Celtic God of knowledge, Dagda, Bridget taught mortals how to whistle. She also brought keening, a mournful singing, to humankind. Representing smithcraft, poetry, inspiration, healing, and medicine, Bridget has a fertility aspect that is associated with Imbolc, the Celtic Festival Day celebrated at the beginning of February. Imbolc is celebrated at a time when the milk of the sheep once again begins to flow after the cold of winter. In some Celtic traditions, Imbolc is known as Bridget's Day, where people light the fires in their hearths while chanting the following verse:

> *Bridget, Bridget, Bridget,*
> *Brightest flame*
> *Bridget, Bridget, Bridget,*
> *Sacred name.*

One of the keys aspects of inspiration is to go with the first idea that inspires you. Go with your intuition, your gut feeling. Don't struggle with it, flow with it instead. Imagine that when it comes to you, your idea is like a river, one that you can float on all the way to a boundless and bottomless ocean of divine creativity. Goddesses of inspiration such as the Celtic Bridget can help you in your voyage to new and uncharted ideas and lands. Use the following three affirmations to give thanks to the Goddess, the one who inspires great creative efforts.

Today I will create a work of art
That is absolutely divine,
Better than anything I've ever done
A creation that lives on through time
Ayea, Great Goddess of creation.
Ayea, Great Lady of inspiration.
Blessed be the Goddess!

Goddess of inspiration, I am One with you.
Today and every day, I feel your protective hand
guiding and helping me give birth to truly divine
creations.

Tonight and every night as I sleep, I call upon the
creative vision of the beloved wise woman.
Spinner of fates and weaver of dreams, please
grant me divine inspiration. So be it!

Actualizing Your Creativity

The most ancient of Greek Goddesses, Eurynome rose from the primordial chaos. Naked, she began dancing in a dance that soon separated light from darkness and the sea from sky. Continuing her dance, Eurynome began swirling in a passion of movement that created a wind-being who pursued her romantically. She grasped the wind in her hand, rolled it like clay into a serpent, and named it Ophion. She mated with the wind serpent, and shape-shifting into a dove, laid the universal egg from which creation hatched. Eurynome of the sea is the mother of all pleasure, whose embodiment is the beautiful triplets. They are the Graces of splendor, abundance, and joyousness.

Ask the Goddess Eurynome to grant you inspiration for art. Perhaps you will even hatch an idea that will become a work of art revered for generations. Art is one way to make your creative spirit live on beyond your own lifetime, much like the Goddess herself. Works of art that stem from divine inspiration are always thought to be far superior to those with more mundane origins. Try this simple affirmation in the evenings before going to sleep.

> *Goddess, I am thankful for your inspiration. I ask*
> *that you help me shape my creation into*
> *something divine. Guide me with your shining*
> *light, tonight and every night.*

The inspiration for creativity can come from the unmanifested, and it is the act of creation that moves it into the manifested to become a work of art. Keep this concept in mind as you do these next two affirmations.

> *From that which has no form*
> *From that which is boundless*
> *Comes an inspiration*
> *That first begins abstractly in my mind*
> *But with the help of the Goddess*
> *Takes shape within the physical world*
> *To become a work of art.*

Out of that which has no name
Comes she who is mother of all things
And from her womb
Comes the creation of all that is
Great Mother of mothers,
Grant me your wisdom and power
That I may have a wondrous life
Always blessed by your divine light.

On Being Creatively Successful

Each year during the first week of August at Lughnassad, the Goddess Rosemerta and her consort Lugh are wedded in a ceremony that marks the end of the growing cycle and beginning of the harvest. Rosemerta, whose name means "the great provider," is the Goddess of prosperity and plenty. Images depicting her show the Goddess sitting on a throne holding the purse of plenty. Rosemerta is also depicted holding a wooden iron-bound bucket, symbolizing regeneration and rebirth, much like the cauldron of renewal that was the forerunner of the Holy Grail.

Each year at Rosemerta's wedding feast, people give thanks for the abundant harvest. What has been sown and grown is then harvested, providing the means for a great feast that gives thanks for the divine hand in it all. You can use affirmations, prayers, and blessings to harvest your creativity and make your work of art a success.

Creation, conception, and birthing are the three faces of creativity. Each project I birth is a divine creation filled with joy and success and blessed by the Goddess.

Today and every day, I am more and more creatively successful. I feel the inspiration of the Goddess, and I am filled with her bright blessings and riches.

Everything is boundless
Everything is unlimited
All obstacles are overcome
All things are possible
With the inspiration of the Goddess
Blessed be.

Oh, Goddess of the harvest,
Blessed be, please inspire me
Let my efforts come to fruition
Ayea! I am creative today
Ayea! I am successful today
Ayea! I am One with the Goddess.

This is the moment that I shine
Brighter than I ever have before
This is the moment that I shine
The divine moment when I am stretching time
With the help of the Goddess of creation.
By the Lady, blessed be!

Living the Creative Life

Goddess of poetry and daughter of Odin, the Norse Goddess Saga is an aspect of the Mother Goddess Frigga. Saga lives at Sinking Beach, where there is a waterfall of cool waves that she offers to her guests in golden cups. Her name means "seeress" and comes from the Norse word for history, and is directly connected to the story of a person's life, more specifically, one's heritage and things spoken of. Thus, Saga is the Goddess of storytellers, those who keep a record of families and clans. As a daughter of Odin, she is a Goddess learned in sacred poetry, charms, and works of power.

The idea in living the creative life is to make your life creative and divine at the same time. You basically write your own life's story or saga, and by being creative about how you live, you can make each day a divine experience. You create the miracles by the choices you make and the actions you take. You create the magic. You are the Goddess! Use the following affirmations to make your own life more creative, full of miracles, and divine inspiration.

> *Goddess, your light surrounds me*
> *And your love enfolds me*
> *Goddess, your creativity inspires me*
> *And your presence watches over me*
> *Everywhere I am, you are there*
> *Blessing me with your everlasting inspiration*
> *That has no boundaries.*
> *Thank you, Great Mother.*

We each weave our lives
With yarns of our own choosing
I choose to live a creative life
At One with the Goddess
The source of all creativity.

Let each day be an inspiration
A connection to the divine
Mother who created us all,
Please lend me a hand
Give me the will to be who I am
Blessed be the Goddess.

I am Oneness
I am divine
I am human
I am humble
From mountains come rocks
From rocks come sand
Washed by the waters of the Goddess
To new and distant lands
Inspire me, Great Lady,
So I may see your many shining faces.
And truly understand my own beauty.

As the sun lights up the moon and planets
So let each one of us light up one another
We are all reflections of the divine light
May we follow the Lady's beacon and find our way home.

May the circle of life
Be forever unbroken
May the Goddess of creation
Always be part of my spirit.

Each day, I resolve to quit letting others take my
personal power away. I take back my power. I am
a creative person who is constantly evolving each
day. I bring in the divine light of the Goddess.
I like the creative person I am, and I like the
spiritual person I am becoming.

Each day is a divine creation
In the loving image of the Goddess
She who is the inspiration of all creation
I ask that the Goddess be One with me today
    and every day.

May I always be in tune
With the powers of creation
From the smallest atom
To the largest cosmos
Everything is Oneness
Everything is divine
Ayea, Bridget!
Ayea, Rosemerta!
Ayea, Kerridwen!
Goddess, bless us all
Blessed be!

☾

CHAPTER SIX

Affirmations, Prayers, and Blessings for Good Health and Vitality

W e all desire good health and vitality because it is a pre-requisite for a better life. To live a long and healthy life is the dream of us all particularly as we get older. It is important to simplify and stick to what's important rather than get stressed out about the little things. More and more studies are coming out saying stress is the number one cause of illness and premature death.

The affirmations, prayers, and blessings in this chapter are meant to help you heal; to cut down on your stress, eat health-ier foods, and start seeing life as an adventure rather than a struggle. When you struggle against your world, you create the "dis-ease" that eventually makes you sick. You must flow in harmony with your world.

The techniques in this book only work when you apply them earnestly. Research in modern psychology has proven that your mind and your thoughts have an affect on the vari-ous aspects of your life. As the practitioner, you have a responsibility to follow the instructions and give the rituals your best concentration.

> *Blessed Lady, Great Goddess,*
> *Through the rays of the sun*
> *Through the waves of the water*
> *Through the Oneness of everything*
> *Purify and revitalize me in every way*
> *Heal my body, mind, and spirit*
> *So be it! Blessed be!*

Your intention, expectation, desire, and rapport with the Goddess are the most important elements for doing successful healing affirmations. I suggest that you begin all healing affirmations by first taking few moments to get in a calm and receptive state of mind. Do this by taking a few deep and complete breaths, relaxing your body and mind and centering yourself. In your mind's eye, imagine exactly the result you want. Then take a few more deep and complete breaths, all the while imagining the best possible healing result. Then read the healing affirmation aloud, like you really mean it!

> *Today, in every situation, I recognize the healing*
> *presence of the Goddess in myself and in those*
> *around me. I call upon her divine wisdom to*
> *heal, bless, and uplift me from the inside out.*

You can also use a modified pulsed-breath technique to enhance the power of healing affirmations. I explain the pulsed-breath method in detail in my book, *The Pocket Guide to Crystals and Gemstones* (Crossing Press). The technique described here is basic but extremely effective when it comes to healing.

Begin by taking a few deep rhythmic breaths. Do this by inhaling to the count of three, holding your breath still for the count of three, and exhaling for three counts. Say the healing affirmation, prayer, or blessing.

Then take another deep breath in. Hold it, and as you do so, imagine the healing already taking place. Next, pulse your breath sharply out through your nose. As you exhale, imagine setting the healthy image in place in your mind's eye. For best results, repeat this pulse-breath healing process three times a day—in the morning, noon, and evening—using the same affirmation, for at least twenty-one days. Your breath acts as a carrier wave for your intention. You are literally breathing the healing into being! Try the pulse-breath method with this simple healing affirmation.

> *Oh, Great Mother, I welcome you into my life*
> *I feel your healing blessings, each and every day!*

In an Egyptian tale, Isis gained power over Ra by sending a snake to bite him. When he became sick from the bite, Ra called upon Isis, renowned for her power to heal, but Isis said the wound was beyond her curative powers by themselves. She told Ra that he must tell her his secret name of power in order to be healed. When he finally relented, he was healed by the Goddess, but her price was eternal power over him.

Use the following affirming blessing when you want to access the healing energy of the Goddess Isis.

May the Goddess bless, heal, and protect me.
I am the serpent queen
The sun's halo
A moonbeam
May the Goddess bless, heal, and protect me.

I am a child of starlight
A sweet melody
A rainbow bright
May the Goddess bless, heal, and protect me.

I am the wind through the trees
A haunting howling
A whispering breeze
May the Goddess bless, heal, and protect me.

I am a dragon's wing
A rainbow
A cool spring
May the Goddess bless, heal, and protect me

Great Mother Goddess, heal me
With wisdom and love
May the Goddess bless, heal, and protect me.
Goddess bless, blessed be the Lady!

Evidence suggests that Isis's original name was "Au Set" which means "spirit." Greeks changed it to Isis. She became the "Lady of Ten Thousand Names," whose true name was Isis. She is the moon, the mother of the sun, culture-bringer, and health-giver. As the first daughter of Nut the sky Goddess, Isis taught people to grind corn, spin flax, and weave cloth.

The following prayer can be used with a group of people. It calls in the healing powers of the Goddess Isis.

> *Dear Isis, Goddess of Creation,*
> *We pray and ask you*
> *To send your healing light among us*
> *Let your healing spirit move within us*
> *And guide us on the path of Oneness.*
> *While we are alive, Great Lady,*
> *We pray and ask you*
> *To help us rise up full of joy*
> *Bless us, Isis, when we die*
> *Let us do so without regret*
> *Always at One with the Goddess.*
> *In our Lady's name, Ayea!*

The Healing Waters of the Goddess

People from all over the ancient world traveled to Bath in England to the healing waters located beside the River Avon at Aquae Sulis. They threw coins and other gifts into the water while asking for the blessing of the healing Goddess Sulis. The springs were hot rather than cold, corresponding to Sulis's association with the Sun. Because her healing powers were widely known and respected, even later when the conquering Romans used the springs, Sulis's name was still put first in dedications to the Goddess.

There is something very healing about warm water, particularly when it springs up from the Earth. Often springs have certain therapeutic minerals that heal if you soak in the waters. The popularity of hot tubs and mineral springs is testament to the healing benefits of warm water. These healing benefits are not limited to the physical body. Because the water helps you to relax and lower your stress level, your mental condition also improves. Today, stress is a major contributing factor to disease and illness. Affirmations, blessings, and prayers can be used to alleviate stress.

Try these next affirmations, prayers, and blessings while immersing yourself in warm water, for example, in a hot spring, hot tub, heated swimming pool, or bathtub. As you recite the words, imagine absorbing all the benefits of the warm water as you release the stress and tension in your body. Take a few deep breaths before and after you say the words while allowing your stress to flow out into the water with your exhaled breaths.

> *I sense my body being revitalized and healthy*
> *I sense my mind full of wonder and the love of life,*
> *I sense my spirit reaching out and connecting to She*
> *Who is the Sun, the Moon, and the Divine Light.*
>
> *I am calm, peaceful, and focused. My body is*
> *relaxing. I am relaxing. I feel the stress flowing*
> *out of my body and being washed away by the*
> *healing waters of the Goddess.*
>
> *With the help of the water Goddess, I am able to*
> *easily restore my energy. My immune system is*

strong and healthy, and every day I feel stronger
than the day before.

As I relax more and more, I feel more connected
with the Goddess. I am a capable, compassionate,
and worthwhile person. Great Goddess, help me
to appreciate myself and like who I am.

I feel the healing energy of the Goddess flowing
into to my _____ (name a specific
part of your body). I am getting stronger,
healthier, and happier each and every day.

I am thankful for my good health. Today and
every day, the divine energy of the Goddess flows
through my body and washes away all of my
stress (depending on the problem, you can
substitute the words "disease" or "pain" instead of
stress).

Goddess of the waters,
Maiden, mother, and crone,
I ask for your blessing
Let your healing energy
Fill me threefold
Surround me with your divine light
Fill me with your love
Ayea, Lady! Blessed be!

Ayea, Great Goddess,

Protectress and healer,
Let your healing waters flow through me
So that I might be whole and healthy.

As an expression of healing energy upon the Earth,
I pray that the Goddess will help me now
Please, Lady, fill me with the divine power
To heal myself and others. Blessed be!

For personal clarity and to help clear your mind of negative thoughts, begin the day with a glass of pure water. Spring or pure well water is the best, but you can use clean tap water if nothing else is available. Ideally, you should drink eight glasses of water a day. Before you drink each glass of water, recite this next affirmation. Drink the water slowly, and as you do, actually imagine (see, feel, and sense) the water cleansing your body of toxins.

Every day, as I drink plenty of clean and delicious
water, it helps clear my mind of unwanted
thoughts. I can feel the healing water of the
Goddess cleansing me and helping my body
release all toxins.

Healthy Eating with the Goddess

Goddess affirmations, blessings, and prayers can be used to reaffirm healthy lifestyle choices. Personal wellness is a unity of body, mind, and spirit, and good health reflects the harmony of this union. Detoxifying and cleansing your body, strengthening your immune system, getting regular exercise, and eating healthful foods are all essential ingredients for healthy living.

An ideal Goddess to work with to create a healthy lifestyle is the Greek "Earth Mother," Demeter. In classical Greece, Demeter was worshiped in fireless ceremonies, at which all offerings were given in their natural state. These offerings included honeycombs, unspun wool, unpressed grapes, and uncooked grain. In this way, she embodied natural rather than artificial production of food. In her role as Goddess of the Earth, she brings order and well-being to both the seasons and human life.

In tune with the Earth Mother, a lot of information has been made readily available to the public about the benefits of eating only natural and organic foods, and staying away from processed and "frankenfoods" (those foods made from genetically engineered crops and animals). Farmers' markets, backyard and neighborhood gardens, health food stores, and natural food co-ops have sprung up in most every town and city, signaling a change in consciousness with regards to healthy eating.

You, too, can tap into the divine energy of the Earth Mother by using affirmations to access her healing power. These affirmations will help you select healthier and more vital natural foods to eat and help you stick to your exercise regime.

I love and care for my body as a sacred vessel. I
select and only eat foods that are healthy for me.

*Today and every day, I am filled with the divine
power of the Goddess. By choosing natural and
living foods to eat, I have plenty of energy to do
my daily activities.*

*I enjoy eating the nourishing vegetables and
fruits of the Earth Goddess. By doing so, I am
able to maintain my ideal weight.*

*I appreciate this nourishing food. It is a sublime
gift from the Goddess that supports and heals me.*

*Each and every day, I love to exercise in many
enjoyable ways. As I exercise, I can feel the power
of the Goddess surging within me, making me
healthier and stronger.*

*As I exercise today, I move in tempo with the
Goddess. I feel her divine energy surrounding
and strengthening me.*

Besides eating more natural foods, more of us are becoming vegetarians. Some individuals choose to be vegetarian because they don't like the idea of killing animals and eating flesh. For example, my son says that animals are our friends, and we don't eat our friends. As a vegetarian family, we don't eat anything with a face.

Others have made the choice to become vegetarian because of high cholesterol, animal fat, hormone-injected meat, or other health considerations. And now, there is "Mad

Cow" disease, which has really tipped the scales in favor of vegetarianism. After all, you are what you eat!

The great Goddess Demeter influences plant life and as a result the health of humans. The following blessings give thanks to the Goddess for the good food she provides us.

Goddess, thank you for this food
May it give me health and well-being
It is from your divine rite that I was born
It is from your fruits and vegetables that I stay alive.
Blessed be the Goddess Demeter. Blessed be!

As I eat this food that comes from the Earth
I give thanks to the Goddess
She who makes this possible
She who makes everything abundant
She who makes everything healthy and vital.
Thank you, Lady, for your nourishing gifts.
Blessed be the Goddess! Blessed be!

Mother, I seek your blessing
You who made me from your womb
I will eat of no flesh
But only from the bountiful harvest
Blessed be the Earth Goddess
She is the source of creation
And thus the great healer
From the One, come the many
From the many, come the One
Ayea, Mother

Ayea, Goddess
Ayea, Oneness.

Goddesses of Fertility and Childbirth

Waterways and bodies of water are traditionally associated with certain Goddesses, who personify water and derive their power from it. These associations go back to the feminine connection with the Moon and its influence on the water element. Celtic Goddesses associated with bodies of water include Boann with the Boyne, Belisama with the Mersey, Sinann with the Shannon, and Coventina with the Carrawburgh in England.

In the particular case of Coventina, who is the Goddess of the holy spring at Brocolitia or Carrawburgh on Hadrian's Wall, people threw coins, jewelry, and figurines into the water as offerings to the Goddess. Women asked Coventina for a safe childbirth. In one drawing of her, she is a water nymph, semi-naked and reclining on lapping waves, holding a water lily in one hand while resting her elbow on an overturned pitcher. In a sculpture, she is seen as a triple nymph, pouring water from an urn.

> *Oh Goddess of the well,*
> *Grant me my wish*
> *Let me conceive and go to term*
> *Let my fetus be healthy,*
> *Oh Goddess of the well,*
> *Grant me my wish*

Let my baby be born divine,
A reflection of you
A reflection of me
A reflection of Oneness.

Ayea, bright blessings to this newborn child
Whose spirit has just emerged from the Mother
We welcome you to this world with love and joy
May you live long, love deeply, and prosper always
I ask this in the Lady's name, Ayea! Blessed be!

Besides being healing and fertility divinities, water and fertility Goddesses are also spirits of inspiration and prophecy. By invoking them into your affirmations, prayers, and blessings, you call upon a power that is multifaceted. This divine power not only helps you in the present with healing and inspiration, but also affects the future with the power of fertility and prophecy, both useful in conceiving and birthing a child as well as for any labor of love that you conceive and to which you give birth.

Goddess, be in my heart
So that I will know love,
Goddess, be in my body
So that I will be fertile,
Goddess, be in my mind
So that I will know what I need to know
Goddess, be in my spirit
So that I will know what is divine
Blessed be the Goddess! Blessed be!

In Chinese mythology, the Goddess who embodies the earth in spring and its fertility is Hu Tu, also called "Empress Earth." Her birthday is celebrated as Mother Earth Day in China on March 8th every year. She can help you integrate nature's wisdom, especially when it comes to pregnancy.

The following fertility prayers are designed to help you conceive and be fruitful. As you say them, walk barefoot on the earth. Also sit on the earth and run the soil through your fingers. Connect as deeply as you can with the earth fertility Goddess as you do this. Feel her sacredness in the ground, and then say these prayers to draw her fertility to you.

Great Goddess, Empress Earth,
I pray you, help me to be fertile
I pray you, help me to be fruitful
I pray you, help me to conceive a healthy child
I ask this with all of my heart
I ask this with my body and soul
I ask this in the Lady's name
So be it! Blessed be!

Dear Goddess, I pray to you, the source of life
Through my prayers, I ask especially for fertility
I pray that you give me your blessing and divine power
So that I may conceive and birth a healthy child.

Dear Goddess, make me an instrument of your fertility
Dear Lady, may the child I bring into the world
Be blessed by your divine love and light

May my child be wanted and filled with hope
Please, Empress Earth Mother, answer my prayers
So be it! Blessed be!

As the Goddess of childbirth and labor, Pi-Hsai Yuan-Chin brings health and good fortune to the newborn and protection to the mother. The princess of the Blue and Purple Clouds, she has six divine helpers, one for each stage of labor. Besides Pi-Hsai Yuan-Chin, she is also known by the names Sheng-mu, "holy mother," Yu Nu, "jade maiden," and T'ien Hsien, "heavenly immortal."

In the spirit of Pi-Hsai Yuan-Chin, the following blessings are for protection of a newborn child and for healing.

Goddess of health
Protect this young soul
Whose journey has just begun
And fill her/him with your divine light.

For this baby
Who has just been born
I ask you, Great Goddess,
For your protection and blessing
So that she/he may always be healthy
And full of life and love
So be it! Blessed be!

Ayea, Goddess of healing, come!
Bless this child with your divine power
Fill this young soul with healing light

So that she/he may be healed of all disease
And live a long, healthy and happy life.
I ask this in the Lady's name. So be it!

The Healing Power of the Earth Goddess

At the stones of Mokosh, named for the Slavic Great Goddess of the Earth, people came to pray for health and prosperity. The crippled and handicapped bring offerings, asking to be whole again.

As the spinner of the thread of life, Mokosh is both the giver of the water of life, as well as the Goddess who takes life. Besides being an Earth Goddess, she is also a Goddess of the rain, which is called Mokosh's milk. She is depicted as a gigantic, horned woman, whose symbol is a circle divided horizontally, representing the Earth with the sky above. Traditionally her name is invoked for aid, strength, and comfort.

I am blessed with rays of sunshine
That make my body grow
Make my mind flower
Make my spirit feel at home
I am blessed with the healing rain
That nourishes my spirit
I thank you, gracious Goddess
You who are mother to us all.

Many spiritual traditions, such as that of the Norse, have stories about how the Goddess spins the divine thread that is then woven into the fabric of each person's life. This fabric is usually divided into past, present, and future.

In terms of health and vitality, this means what you did, ate, and thought in the past affects your present health, and what you are doing now affects how healthy you are now and will be in the future. Be good to your body, and your body will be good to you. In this sense, your body is like the Earth. It reflects the way you treat it. If you plant healthy seeds, cultivate and water them with care, your harvest will be fruitful and healthy.

The following blessings invoke the power of the Earth Mother as the giver of life, insurer of health, and weaver of the future. It is her light that illuminates you when you enter your period of florescence, which can last anywhere from the Andy Warhol "fifteen minutes of fame" for some people, to a lifetime for others. The choice is yours to make. Don't let your dreams die for lack of water.

> *Tonight and every night,*
> *May the Great Goddess grant me*
> *Vitality, personal power, well-being, and healing*
>   *dreams*
> *I know that all aspects of my life*
> *Are getting healthier and becoming more positive*
> *Dream it so! Blessed be!*
>
> *Mother, I feel your healing light*
> *As you gently touch my soul*
> *I know that everything will be all right*

With you in my life,
I am whole again
Blessed be the Mother
Blessed be the Goddess
Who is Mother of all things.

I am a flower
And the Goddess is the earth
She is the water that gives me life
When I bloom with vitality
It is in her reflection that I become divine.

Goddess, bathe me in your blue light
So that all negativity will leave my body
Goddess, bathe me in your green light
So that positive new patterns will grow
Goddess, bathe me in your golden light
So that I might be healed forever more,
Goddess, bathe me in your white light
So that I may become divine
Ayea! So be it!

Protecting Your Health

Like many of the Celtic Goddesses of health, Epona, the horse
Goddess, is associated with sacred waters, and as such, many
of her shrines were situated close to thermal springs. Besides
being a Goddess of springs, streams, and rivers, Epona is the
Goddess who travels with the soul on its final journey beyond

death. She is Goddess of healing and fertility who protects and nurtures animals.

> *Oh Great Goddess,*
> *Protector of my life,*
> *I know you're always with me*
> *Wherever I go.*

Like a watch dog that barks at every intruder, this aspect of the Goddess protects you from disease. Disease disrupts your normal progression to the point where you are sick and become tired of what's happening in your life.

In the natural world, the plants with less water or fewer nutrients are the most prone to disease and illness. In human terms, this means you need water and nutrients to stay alive.

The following is a basic blessing for ridding your personal space of any unwanted energies. You can add power to this blessing by smudging with sage and cedar or sweetgrass while you say the words.

> *May all evil and foulness be gone from this place*
> *I ask this in our Lady's name.*
> *Bless this place, Great Goddess, now and forevermore.*
> *Ayea!*

Now imagine that you are bathing in a clear, pure mountain stream. Feel the stream running through your being, washing everything clean. With this image in your mind, say the following.

Goddess, purify my life's waters
So that they flow freely from the source
Let me be free from disease
Forever bless me, dear Lady!

Iris, the female counterpart to Hermes/Mercury, brought the healing power of the Mother Goddess to earth via a rainbow carrying the caduceus, which symbolizes wholeness. Hermes took the staff and taught healing to Asklepios, son of Apollo, who taught his daughter Hygiea, whose Roman counterpart was Salus, Goddess of preserving good health.

One of Hygiea's sisters was Meditrina, who was associated with restoring good health. Meditrina, whose name means healer, is the Roman Goddess of medicine, wine, and health. In Rome, every year on October 11th, the Meditrinalia, one of the festivals connected with the cultivation of the vineyards, is held to honor the Goddess Meditrina. One of the practices is to pour an offering of new and old wine, and then toast the Goddess with the Latin words, "Vetus novum vinum bibo, novo veteri morbo medeor," meaning,

Wine new and old I drink,
Of illness new and old I'm cured.

You can use these affirmations to help you access the healing power of Meditrina to restore your mental, physical, and spiritual health.

My heart is opening to loving myself as I love the
Goddess. With trust and faith in the Lady and in

*myself, I feel my energy and good health being
restored each and every day.*

*With the helping hand of the Goddess, I practice
only good habits and eat those foods that restore
my health and promote body, mind, and spirit
wellness. I enjoy taking charge of my life.*

*Tonight and every night, the healing power of the
Goddess's love is within me. I let go of worry and
regrets. I open my heart and feel healed and
restored as I sleep and dream, waking refreshed
and joyful.*

You can use this prayer to ask the Goddess to help restore your
mind, body, and spirit.

*In the house of dawn's healing light
By the divine powers of the Goddess of Earth
Her feet, my feet restore
Her limbs, my limbs restore
Her body, my body restore
Her mind, my mind restore
Her spirit, my spirit restore
Her voice, my voice restore
Her aura, my aura restore
With beauty before her, with beauty before me
With beauty behind her, with beauty behind me
With beauty above her, with beauty above me
With beauty below her, with beauty below me*

With beauty around her, with beauty around me
With fragrance beautiful in her voice,
With fragrance beautiful in my voice
She is healed in beauty, I am healed in beauty
In the house woven in the evening's healing light
Bless you, Great Goddess, now and forevermore.

Bastet, also known as Bast, mentioned in chapter 3, is the Egyptian Goddess of fertility and protection. She is gentle most of the time, and depicted as a cat or as a woman with a cat's head. For those few times when she is angry, Bast shifts from a cat shape into the lion Goddess, Sckhmet. As the lioness, she is the Great Protector. Bastet carries a sistrum with her, which is a rattle with four strings that she uses to scare off evil spirits, making her a good Goddess to use for protection, particularly from illness.

Bastet is also associated with the moon, the heavenly body that greatly influences all water, including healing waters and the water in your body. Traditionally, Bastet is known for bestowing both physical and mental health to those who receive her blessings.

The following affirmations ask for the Goddess's blessings to heal and protect you from disease. Remember if you prefer, go ahead and substitute the name of another healing Goddess for Bast.

O Great Goddess, Bast,
Mother of all things,
Unite my body with your divine spirit

And make me whole again,
O Great Protector, Bast,
Mother of all things,
Unite my mind with your divine spirit
And make me whole again,
O Great Goddess, Bast,
Mother of all things,
Unite my soul with your divine spirit
And make me whole again.

Great Goddess,
Who gives life to all life,
Let your healing waters wash through me
Cleansing me of all illness
And healing my wounds
You are my true self
Luminous and wonderful
Awakening my spirit
On a daily basis
From its ancient slumber.

Goddess, bless me with the power
To remember who I really am
I am a child of light
Goddess, bless me with the ability to help heal others
And heal myself.

Blessed Lady,
Please protect me from evil
That sometimes tries to come into my home

Please protect me from the illness
That sometimes tries to invade my body
Let me be healthy and strong
And always within your blessings.

Depicted as the thousand-armed and thousand-eyed Chinese Goddess, Kuan Yin is a motherly figure often called upon in times of danger. Originally an Indian Princess and Buddhist bodhisattva, she turned back from the gates of heaven when she heard someone on earth cry. She then vowed to stay on earth to help ease humankind's suffering.

Queen of Heaven,
Lady of Compassion,
I trust you to always protect me from harm
I will not fear, for you are always here
And you will ever be by my side.
May I nurture a sense of infinite love
I ask this in our Lady's name
Blessed be!

Celebrating Healing

Normally after doing rituals for the Goddess, it is customary to do healings and to toast the Goddess with either wine or fruit juice, depending on your preference. Healings are usually done by chanting the Goddess's name repeatedly while envisioning the focus of the healing, either yourself or another person of your choosing, as being healed and free from disease. Once again, it is important to keep your healing intentions clear and directed. The toast that comes afterward is an offering of thanks to the Goddess, for her help in the healing.

After doing each of the following healing affirmations, give thanks to the Goddess by toasting her with a glass of wine or fruit juice. When toasting, hold your glass high in the air, and say, "Ayea, Meditrina, Ayea, Epona, Ayea, Mokosh, Ayea, Pi-Hsai Yuan-Chin, Ayea, Demeter, Ayea, Sulis, Ayea, Isis, Ayea, Kuan Yin!" You can toast all of the Goddesses or you can toast one, two, or three of them. There are no rules. Just follow your intuition.

As you drink the wine or juice, feel the healing energy of the Goddess entering your body, healing you with her divine powers.

> *Come, Goddess of healing,*
> *Let each part of my body feel your healing light*
> *Let every cell be revitalized with your love.*
>
> *I feel the light of the Goddess moving through and*
> *healing every part of my body, healing every part*
> *of my mind, healing every part of my spirit. I feel*
> *a sense of complete well-being. Thank you, Lady.*
> *I drink to your divine wisdom and love.*
>
> *I celebrate the blessings of the Goddess. Bless you,*
> *Lady, for all of your divine gifts.*

A simple but sacred way to celebrate the Goddess is to take a day off in her honor. When the weather permits and you don't have other commitments, spend a day, morning, or afternoon alone. Make an effort to drink only water and eat only fresh organic fruits during this time. Spend the time doing simple things that you enjoy, such as singing, playing music, writing poetry, just thinking about things, reading, and being in nature. A long, leisurely walk in the country or by the ocean would be perfect. Or go outside and pick flowers or hunt for special rocks. Throughout the day, repeat these powerful affirmations, now and again.

I am awakening the divine power of the Goddess within me, every moment of every day.

Mother Goddess, full of grace, I celebrate your love.

My heart is the heart of the Goddess. My heart is open. My eyes are the eyes of the Goddess. My eyes are open. My soul is the soul of the Goddess. My soul is divine. We are One.

☾

CHAPTER SEVEN

Affirmations, Prayers, and Blessings for Abundance and Attaining Goals

*T*he Celtic Goddess, Anu (Danu), represents the energies of manifestation, fertility, and prosperity. She is a Mother Goddess closely associated with the land. Two breast-shaped mountains in County Kerry in Western Ireland are called "Dá Chích Anann," translated as "the paps of Anu." Anu is known to be one of the Dea Matronae of Ireland, and in the night sky she appears as Llys Don, more commonly known as the constellation Cassiopeia. She is also known as the Goddess Aine, to whom fires were lit on Midsummer's Eve, and who was the guardian of cattle, a symbol of wealth in Celtic society.

Anu can help you create more wealth and abundance in your life when you fashion something creative from the elements around you. In gardening, this means taking a seed, putting it in soil, giving it water and light, and watching it grow. The seed is your intention or idea of what you would like to create. The water and light reflect your desire and efforts in the process. For example, one of your efforts is doing the affirmations in this book for prosperity. Merging with the Goddess ignites the divine element in the formula, and makes it all happen!

> *Goddess, today I ask for your blessings*
> *So that my garden will grow abundant*
> *From the fruits of my labors*
> *And the grace of your divine hand.*
> *By the Lady, blessed be!*

> *Great Goddess Anu, I pray and ask that your*
> *blessings of prosperity and abundance be*
> *bestowed upon me and those I love. Thank you*
> *for your divine gifts. Ayea!*

Before doing the following affirmations, think about your opinions on prosperity and abundance, which are different for each person. Prosperity and abundance must work naturally into your life in order to come in at all. The water is fine, but before you dive in, I suggest that you test out the temperature on things like a new house in a new town or a new profession. Check things out first. Try to form a clear picture of what you want, and then make certain that you really want it.

> *I ask for and receive abundance and prosperity*
> *every day. As my inner light shines brighter,*
> *positive energy flows through me, and I can feel*
> *the helping hand of the Goddess.*

> *I enjoy tapping into the divine boundlessness of*
> *universal abundance. I savor the moment like a*

fine meal, knowing as one moment ends, another
begins, making my life a exquisite adventure.

Today and every day, I invite and accept the
overflowing abundance and love of the Goddess
into my life.

I have the natural Goddess-given power to attract
prosperity and success into my daily life, easily
and effortlessly, freely and abundantly.

Three faces of Anu are Earth Ana, Moon Ana, and Sun Ana, translating back into those garden ideas of earth, water, and light and magical ideas of intention, desire, and merging. This powerful three-step affirmation technique can be successfully used by everyone.

1. Write on the back of your business card, or on a 3x5 index card, the words, "Goddess Bless! I am so happy that I am _____." You fill in the blank with your goal, which might be to establish a schedule for financial independence; to secure one new contract a month; to meet one new client every day; to attract prosperity through good works; or to help yourself and others live more abundant lives by doing what you love to do.

2. Carry the card with you during the day. Read it over three times to yourself. Better yet, read it out loud, if possible, five times during the day: 1) upon awakening, 2) at breakfast, 3) at lunch, 4) at dinner, and 5) just before you go to sleep. Do

this for a week. Then try it for a month, a few months, a year, and then, continuously throughout your life.

3. You will discover the more you do this and the more you become one with the statement on the card, the faster your goals will manifest in your life.

The Ancient Runes of the Goddess

The Runes are powerful, ancient Norse symbols that can be used to connect with the Goddess. The power of the first rune of the Norse Elder Futhark, Fehu, can be used to bring more abundance and prosperity into your life. It is the eldest rune, and looks either like the horns of a cow or two arms reaching skyward in what is called the Goddess stance.

In Norse mythology, Fehu is associated with both the Norse Aesir, the deities of humankind, and the Vanir, the deities of nature. More specifically, the feminine side of this rune relates to the Goddess Freya and her mother the Goddess Nerthus. These women represent fertility and the natural wealth of the Earth

Coming directly out of the creation of the universe, Fehu's power is raw archetypal energy. It is the power of motion and expansion. In Norse mythology, this force flows from Muspelheim, the southern world of flames. It acts as the source of the cosmic fire, from which Midgard, our human world, was created.

Interestingly, the cosmic fire illustrated by Fehu not only represents creation but also destruction, again reflecting the energetic polarities inherent in things, including personal prosperity.

Throughout the history of humankind, Goddesses of abundance such as Freya have often shown their generous nature by answering affirming prayers. There have been many times in my life when I have needed money to pay unexpected bills, and the Goddess has been there to help me again and again.

Great Goddess Freya, I pray you
Please help me to ask for what I truly want
Help me to take decisive action
Grant me persistence and patience
Give me strength and confidence in myself
Help me joyfully attain my goals
Help me to build loving relationships
Show me how to create a healthier balance
Show me the larger picture
And help me to live with purpose
I ask this in the name of the Goddess Freya,
So be it! Blessed be!

May the divine abundance of the blessed Mother
Goddess be with me, and those I love, now and
forever more. Goddess bless us and protect us.
Blessed be!

Great Goddess, I pray you
Please bless me with your divine gifts of abundance

I am you as you are She and together we are One.
By the Lady, blessed be!

The original meaning of Fehu derives from cattle, which originally meant mobile wealth and the power that came from it. Today, mobile wealth comes in the form of money, which buys goods that can be bartered and sold.

In the early Goddess cultures such as the Norse and the Celtic, cattle were kept and milked, thus providing a constant source of food. Cattle could also be sold or bartered for other goods and killed for meat. Their hides could be used for clothing, their bones and horns for tools, and their fat for candles.

The first letter of the Hebrew, Greek, and Gothic alphabets also means cattle, illustrating the importance of these animals in the lives of people living in these early societies. Cattle came to symbolize wealth and fertility. Because of this, Goddesses of abundance often have a bovine connection or aspect to them.

You can harness the abundant power of these Goddesses through affirmations, prayers, and blessings.

Goddess, who is all things to all people
Grant me your blessing
So that I might know what abundance is
Now and forever more.

I am thankful for the money that the Goddess provides,
plenty of money to support and sustain me.

*The divine love of the Goddess uplifts me every
moment of every day. Her loving presence helps
me attain remarkable success and prosperity.*

*Today and every day, I imagine myself working
toward goals that produce wonderful results.
I perceive myself as a successful and prosperous
person.*

Akin to the concept of the Mother Goddess, the F-rune, Fehu, rules the basic force of fertility, containing the mystery of both creation and destruction. From the primordial fires come the waters of life. From the fertility of the land comes the breath of the divine. These extremes, creation and destruction, are the polarities that, like wealth, can either create or destroy, depending upon the situation.

Fehu defines a mobile form of energy closely related to the Germanic concept of "hamingia," which translates as good luck and guardian spirit. The "hamingia" is an energy projected from a person like that of the astral body. As an energy force, Fehu embodies the directed, expansive power that moves energy outward from people and objects. This power manifests when you do affirmations, prayers, and blessings.

Besides the horns of cow, the two lines on the F-rune extending upward also look like a person with his or her hands raised and outstretched. This is traditionally called the Goddess position and is used by priests and priestesses for prayers and blessings. In this way, Fehu symbolizes communing with the Goddess, where a person's field of intention moves outward (and inward) into the many dimensions of Oneness.

The energy of the F-rune is the unbridled creative fire that has no boundaries and no real structure or form. This energy intimidates some people because of its uncontrollable nature. But if you merge with the Fehu energy and become One with it, you receive a great burst of creative fire that can be used to create more abundance and prosperity in your life. For more ways to use runes for affirmation and prayer, plus runic correspondences to the Goddesses, please refer to my book, *The Little Giant Encyclopedia of Runes* (Sterling Press).

Do this next affirmation at half-past noon, the time traditionally associated with Fehu. Like the "Fe, Fi, Fo, Fum" spoken by the giant in the tale "Jack and the Beanstalk," the chant of this affirmation is also based on an ancient runic song called the "Galdr."

Fehu, Fehu, Fehu
Fu, fa, fi, fe, fo
Energize each part of my body,
Fehu, Fehu, Fehu
Fa, fi, fe, fo, fu
Enlighten each part of my mind,
Fehu, Fehu, Fehu
Fi, fe, fo, fu, fa
Bless each part of my spirit
So that I may have an abundant life
And know the divine light of the Goddess.

The Sisters of Destiny

In the Norse Tradition, the Norns are the three sisters who control the destiny of everyone and everything. The first sister, Urd, creates patterns by taking energy from the divine and handing it to the second, Verdandi, who then begins to weave it into physical matter. Verdandi hands the weave to Sculd who then unravels it and tosses the threads of life back into the abyss of the divine. The Norns move energy the same way as do the Three Fates from classical Greek mythology: from the unmanifested (divine) into the manifested (mortal), and back again into the unmanifested (divine). It's a never-ending cycle. This is why the Fates are the origin of all Goddesses, and for that matter, all life.

In terms of prosperity and abundance, the Norns represent the source and flow of all creation, including any type of wealth and good fortune. These divine women are three of the most powerful Goddesses that you can ask for help, guidance, blessing, and protection. The only thing they ask of you is that you be completely and utterly honest when you are working with them.

Three sisters,
Administrators of my fate,
I ask for your blessings
So that my life will always be abundant.

Dear Goddesses of Fate, bless me
May I be happy and mindful

Dear Goddesses of destiny, guide me
May I care for myself with joy
Dear Goddesses of destiny, protect me
Please keep me safe
Dear Goddesses of destiny, love me
May I learn from your wisdom
Dear Goddesses of Fate, bless me
Now and forever more.

The Three Fates epitomize the saying "if it was meant to be, it will be." Unlike the "grab them by the balls, and their minds and hearts will follow" philosophy, the Fates suggest that we all have a personal destiny, a special purpose in life to fulfill while we are here in physical form upon the Earth.

When you follow your calling into your deepest desires and into what you really feel is right for you in your heart and head, you will find that life is more satisfying, exciting, and joyful. Don't just settle for life, live it to its fullest!

May the Goddess weave wealth, abundance, and
love into my life today and every day. By the
Lady, blessed be!

Thank you, Goddess, for opening the doors to
opportunity for me. Now that they are opened, I
am successfully working toward my goals.

Great Lady, help me to continually exceed the
expectations of my clients (customers). May I

serve others gently, with love, wisdom, and compassion. So be it. Blessed be!

My goals are aligned with a well-defined sense of purpose. I enjoy peace of mind and a wonderful feeling of being alive and in step with destiny.

With the guiding light of the Goddess, my life's purpose becomes clear and my life has rich meaning.

By the grace of the Fates, I live my life to its fullest. I weave my goals, like brilliant threads, into the fabric of life, and I easily attain them through wise and diligent effort.

By the Lady, I now have the energy, wisdom, time, and enough money to fulfill my deepest desires.

With the helpful hand of the Goddess, I am gathering the skills and like-minded colleagues to help me make my dreams come true right now.

The Many Faces of Abundance

An ancient Egyptian Goddess who existed in predynastic times, Hathor, was identified with many local Goddesses. In a sense, all the Goddesses were Hathor in one form or another. She is a Goddess of abundance with many powerful faces: Sky-

Goddess, Sun-Goddess, Moon-Goddess, Goddess of the east, Goddess of the west, Goddess of moisture, fertility Goddess, agricultural Goddess, and a Goddess of the Underworld.

Hathor also has many names. She is called the Mistress of Life, the Great Wild Cow, the Golden One, the Mistress of Turquoise, and the Lady of Dendera, as well as the Lady of Punt, the Powerful One, the Mistress of the Desert, and Lady of the Southern Sycamore. Because of this, she is also called the Seven Hathors. Traditionally worshipped in the seven cities of Thebes, Heliopolis, Aphroditopolis, Sinai, Momemphis, Herakleopolis, and Keset, the Seven Hathors are linked to the Pleiades.

In one Egyptian myth, when the hero is born, the Seven Hathors, who disguise themselves as seven young women, appear and announce his fate. This is not only a matter of fortune-telling, as the Seven Hathors also act as questioners of the soul on its way to the Land of the West. You can use the following seven-versed prayer to bring the Hathor's power into your daily life.

> *Dear Goddess, bless us*
> *May we be happy and prosperous*
> *Dear Goddess, guide us*
> *May we care for ourselves with joy*
> *Dear Goddess, help us*
> *May we attain our deepest desires*
> *Dear Goddess, protect us*
> *May we be safe from harm*
> *Dear Goddess, teach us*

May we learn from your wisdom
Dear Goddess, love us
May we feel your love every moment
Dear Goddess, bless us
Now and forevermore.

As with the Celts and the Norse, the Egyptians also perceived cattle as a symbol of prosperity and abundance. Because of this, Hathor is depicted as a woman with cow's horns with the sun between them, or as a beautiful woman with cow's ears, or as a cow wearing the sun disk between her horns.

In her role as a Goddess of fertility and moisture, Hathor is associated with the Dog Star, Sirius, whose rising above the horizon heralded the annual flooding of the Nile. She is often depicted as a nurturer and is said to be the divine mother of the Pharaoh.

You can use the power of affirmation and prayer to access Hathor's divine energy.

Today, I choose to dwell on thoughts of love,
peace, and harmony. May the Powerful One help
me to acknowledge and express my power of
choice moment by moment, and to keep my mind
turned in a positive, peaceful, and productive
direction.

Mistress of Life, Golden One,
Goddess of the West and East,
Hear me now, divine Lady,

Please grant me wisdom
Please grant me wealth
Please grant me love
May your abundant blessings
Shine upon me and those I love
Now and forevermore.

Besides being a Goddess of motherhood, Hathor is the protectress of pregnant women and patron of all women. As the "Mistress of the Necropolis" she has the head of a cow that protrudes from the side of a mountain. She wears a menat necklace, the symbol of rebirth.

Great Mother, may your fertile and fruitful
power now manifest in my life. Thank you for
your kind generosity. Blessed be!

Today and every day, may the loving and fertile
presence of the Goddess work through me to
bring resolution to all money matters in my life,
and to help me discover personal success and
prosperity.

Abundance Begins at Home

The Roman Goddess Vesta is strongly associated with fire. In fact, she is fire, and in turn, fire is Vesta. In her temple on the Palatine Hill, the sacred fire of the Roman state burned continually, only extinguished and relit once a year on March 1, the beginning of the Roman year. Vesta's sacred festival was the Vestalia, held from June 7 to June 15. On the first day of the festival, barefoot women brought offerings of food baked on their hearths. On the last day of Vestalia, the temple was ritualistically cleansed, thus renewing the energy for another year.

Vesta is a Goddess of the hearth and home. In ancient Rome, this made her the central divinity of the family. She was honored as Goddess of motherhood, and as such, viewed as a symbol of the continued renewal of the family and the people.

> *Thank you, Lady, for your gifts of food, clothing,*
> *and shelter, for helping me have a happy home*
> *and to live a comfortable and prosperous life.*
> *May you always bless me with your abundance.*

> *Mother Goddess, I ask that your abundant and*
> *loving nature manifest within my life, each and*
> *every day. As I will, so shall it be. Blessed be!*

> *I feel the creative fire of the Goddess fueling my*
> *deepest desires and helping me attain my*
> *personal goals.*

> *The green fire of the Goddess fills me with*
> *brilliant abundance and prosperity.*

The fire in Vesta's temple, which symbolized the Roman state, was tended by the vestals: young women between the ages of six and ten chosen from the finest of Rome's elite families. The vestals came into the service of the Goddess in childhood and took a vow of virginity and service for thirty years. When a vacancy occurred in the college of vestals, a new girl was chosen, and admitted with the words, "I take you; you shall be the priestess of Vesta, and you shall fulfill the sacred rites for the safety of the Roman people."

> *Dear Goddess, I ask that you bless and guide me and those I love every day. Please help us live long and fruitful lives. Blessed be, Great Provider!*

> *By the grace of the Goddess, I am helping as many people as I can during my lifetime in a way that significantly improves their lives.*

> *The divine light of the Goddess shines within me. Each and every day, I share her brilliance with everyone I meet.*

At One with the Laws of Nature

Artemis is a Greek Goddess of fruitful abundance. Called the "Lady of the Beasts," she is the huntress who protects animals, and as such, represents the primal instincts of animals. She is also a tree, a bear, and the moon. She symbolizes a woman moving through the cycles of life. She is ruler of the nymphs and represents the instinct to live, produce, and reproduce, signifying the laws of nature rather than the laws of society. The laws of nature are as ancient and everlasting as the Goddess herself.

I live in accordance with the laws of nature
Which came into being with the creation of the
   Goddess
She, who is all things, both the Sun and Moon
She, whose body is that from which we all draw life.

The Goddess empowers me.
My work empowers me,
I empower those around me.
Blessed be!

Goddess of abundance,
Let every seed I plant grow fruitful
Blessed and protected by your light
Let my garden grow from one year to the next
Renewed each year by the your divine spirit
By the Lady, blessed be!

The Goddess of Compassion and Generosity

Ezili is a Haitian Goddess who is generous to the point of extravagance. She goes by many names: Ezili Ge-Rouge, the fury of a scorned woman; Maitresse, the femme fatale who grieves at the inability of the world to conceive beyond reality and to desire beyond adequacy; and Ezili Freda Dahomey, the virgin who looks at the experience of life with freshness.

Ezili's symbols include a heart, roses, jewelry, and flamingoes. She represents luxury, sensuality, and generosity, and likes offerings of perfume, creme de cacao, champagne, and sweet foods. She is bountiful, capable, compassionate, and a protector of children and the less fortunate.

Lady of roses,
Your spirit is dear to me
I love your fragrant smile
And your priceless love.

The Great Lady provides plenty of money for all the things I need. I intend to be financially independent in _____ years. I will earn _____ dollars this year. So be it!

Today I share my abundance with those I love. I feel the capable and compassionate power of the Goddess filling and refreshing me.

With the helping hand of the Goddess, I am attaining my heartfelt goals each and every day.

Physical and Spiritual Abundance

The Hindu Goddess Lakshmi embodies all forms of wealth. Her essence is in jewels, in rare shells, in every child born to welcoming parents, and particularly in cows. A mythological tale conveys how she sprang up from the ocean adorned with necklaces and pearls. She symbolizes not only the wealth of the Earth but also the wealth of the soul, signifying the delights of spiritual prosperity and how the physical and spiritual are balanced together.

In Hindu spirituality, male energy tends to be passive and abstract, distant and powerless, unless activated by the feminine. Lakshmi's mate, Vishnu, only has the power to maintain and enrich life when she inspires it. Existing through all of time, and floating before the dawn of creation on a lotus, Lakshmi is also called Padma, "lotus-Goddess," the lotus being a symbol of spiritual enlightenment.

The following affirmations can be used to attract more wealth and spiritual abundance into your life.

*Newfound abundance and prosperity from the
lotus Goddess are flowing effortlessly into my life
today and every day.*

*With the helping hand of the Lady, I work through the
difficulties, challenges, and problems along the way. In
doing so, I create a path for spiritual abundance and
wealth to flow into my life.*

*Thank you, Goddess, for helping me learn from
my failures, and for giving me the strength and
insight to leave them in the past. Thank you,
Goddess, for helping me to build upon my
strengths and successes and for giving me the
ability to bring newfound abundance into my life
right now.*

I enjoy each facet of the work that I do. Every day I draw the spiritual abundance of the many-jeweled Goddess into my life by doing what I love with passion and excellence.

With the grace of the Goddess, I inspire and empower people to live their highest vision with love, harmony, and joy.

I am thankful that every day, another divine opportunity comes my way.

By the Lady's hand, I willingly give to others in need.

With the divine love of the Lady and a happy heart, I focus on what I do best, and do it very well indeed.

I invite the opportunities and divine gifts that complement and expand my greatest strengths into my life right now.

At my core, I feel I matter and make a difference in the world. I feel the wisdom and love of the Goddess guiding and inspiring me each and every day.

Tonight and every night, I am at peace with myself and those around me. I am in harmony with the universe. My life is filled with the loving abundance of the divine Goddess. I know we are One.

☾

CHAPTER EIGHT

Affirmations, Prayers, and Blessings for Peace and Harmony

Last night, I sang a song of peace
So that the whole world might hear
Time to put away the guns
Time to learn to live as One.

☽

*H*alcyon days are a time of calm weather that extends from seven days before to seven days after the winter solstice. The halcyon (kingfisher) builds her nest on the calm water, which contrasts with the prevailing patterns of winter storms. The reason for this calmness is the Goddess, who grants a stilling of the weather, creating a period of peace and harmony within a world of stormy chaos. Within this momentary stillness, the halcyon hatches and rears her young.

In Greek mythology, when the Goddess Halcyone was still a mortal woman, she had a dream where she saw her beloved, the fisherman Ceyx, perishing at sea. Her nightmare happened. Watching by the water's edge, she retrieved Ceyx's body as the waves carried it to shore. Through her grief and longing for her lover, she shape-shifted into the first kingfisher and in the process magically revived Ceyx, who also shape-shifted into a kingfisher.

The Greek Goddesses and Gods saw the love that the couple had for one another and so in turn blessed them with good weather, so that now when kingfisher goes to lay her eggs, a calm moves across the waters until the eggs are hatched. So the halcyon days were born.

Like the legendary kingfisher, we all need times of calm and peace just to keep our sanity. Affirmations, prayers, and blessings are natural ways to bring peace and harmony into our lives. Repeating something over and over has a built in calming effect, so try repeating these affirming words and passages to soothe and comfort.

> *Today, I choose to dwell on thoughts of love,*
> *peace, and harmony. May the Great Goddess help*
> *me to acknowledge and express my power of*
> *choice moment by moment, and to keep my mind*
> *turned in a positive, peaceful, and productive*
> *direction.*
>
> *Goddess, grant me a period of calm*
> *Where the forces around me*
> *Move in peace and harmony*
> *Where the struggle ends*
> *And the divinity begins.*
> *By the Goddess, blessed be!*

Mother, I remember when I was a part of you
Inside your belly, before I was born,
Even though we have seemingly separated into two
*   beings*
Energetically we will always be One.

The Compassionate Goddess

In China, Kuan Yin is honored in every home as the most powerful being in the entire Chinese divinity. It is said that her empathy and compassion were so great that when she received enlightenment, she chose to remain in human form rather than transcend as pure energy. She will stay in her human form until every living creature attains enlightenment, and in the meantime she answers every prayer addressed to her.

To speak Kuan Yin's name in prayer assures salvation from physical and spiritual harm. As a testament to her peace and mercy, her most devout worshipers eat no flesh and live entirely without doing violence to other beings. Chief symbol of human compassion, she makes symbolic gestures of generosity and banishes fear and hardship. The most effective meditation is the constant repetition of Kuan Yin's name, bringing continual inner peace and a feeling of generosity into every aspect of your life. We are the Goddess in a spiritual sense. We are parts of her many aspects. As our mother, she exists as a part of us all.

I am peace
I am prosperity

I am the Oneness
That unites us
I am love
I am beauty
I am the Oneness
That unites us.

Human beings
Are what we are
A creation of the Goddess
A shining star.

As I breathe in
I see an image of the Goddess
As I breathe out
All of my stress goes out the window.

Balance as the Key to Peace and Harmony

The Egyptian Goddess Maat, whose name means "that which is straight," represents the ideas of law, order, and truth. She is an ancient Goddess because of her role in the boat of Ra as it rose above the waters of the abyss of Nu on the first day. One of her other names is the "eye of Ra," and she is depicted as a woman wearing a tall ostrich feather, or sometimes as simply an ostrich feather.

Maat's association with the ostrich feather comes from a passage in *The Book of the Dead*, where the judgment of the dead is done in the Hall of Maat. The heart or conscience of the dead person is weighed against the feather of Maat, and if it is balanced then the spirit of the dead person could mingle freely with the divine. In this sense, Maat embodies not only that which is true and ordered, but also that which is balanced.

The idea of being in balance with the world around you plays an important role in bringing peace and harmony into your life. Like the scales that represent the sun sign Libra, balance happens on many levels at once, and if one aspect goes out of balance, the overall imbalance affects all your life's aspects. An example would be when you become overly angry or stressed out because of your job. What starts as a mental problem or imbalance bleeds over into the physical, and begins to manifest itself as ailments in your body.

The important thing is to keep the balance in your life, and not let one aspect get out of control. You can use affirmations to keep that balance.

> *Goddess of Earth and Air,*
> *Goddess of Fire and Water,*
> *Let all the elements in my life*
> *Be balanced and in harmony with one another.*

Part of being at peace with yourself is being true to who you are; otherwise you are always rubbing against the grain in frustration and stress. Try to keep your head about you when everyone else is losing theirs. Connecting with the Goddess can empower you and help you stay sane in the modern world.

*Tonight and every night, I am at peace with
myself and those around me. I am in harmony
with the universe. I am empowered by the love of
the divine Goddess. I know we are One in spirit.*

Bringing Unity and Harmony into your Life

If you think your parents didn't get along, the Greek Goddess
Harmonia, known as the "uniter," had Aphrodite, the Goddess
of love, as her mother, and Aries, the God of war, as her father.
Talk about opposites attracting! At Harmonia's marriage ceremony, all the Olympians came bearing magical gifts, including a necklace from Aphrodite that made anyone who wore it
sexually irresistible.

Harmonia, Goddess of music, dance, and poetry, is
depicted as a lovely, silver-haired Goddess who is gentle, kind,
and much beloved by the gods. She could put anyone at peace
with her music, giving substance to the saying, "Music soothes
the savage beast." Music is all about the harmony of notes that
make up the whole of the composition. Peace and harmony is
all about the relationships of people that make up the whole of
Oneness.

The following three affirmations express these ideas of
peace and harmony. Take a few deep breaths to center yourself
before beginning. As you say each one, imagine yourself at
complete harmony with everything around you and at peace
with the world.

Goddess of Peace,
Divine daughter,
I pray you
Unite us all
Help us to know peace
Help us to know beauty
Help us to know love
Help us to know harmony
May all be well in the world
By the Goddess, blessed be!

I have felt the forces of war
Now let me feel peace
I have felt the anger and hatred
Now let me feel love
One step beyond war is peace
One step beyond hatred is love
I know I need to make that extra step
To be at One with the world.

Today and every day, I am more honest with
those around me, and they are more loving in
return. I am One with the divine feminine, and I
express anger in appropriate ways so that peace
and harmony are the result.

Because she takes no human form, Hestia never has any statues erected in her honor. As the fire of the hearth, living in the
center of every home, she honors guests who are beneficial to
those she blesses.

Hestia symbolizes family unity, and as such embodies the basic social contract. As the firstborn of the Olympian Goddesses, Hestia inspired a tradition in which a new home was not fully established until a woman brought fire from her mother's hearth to light her own, thus beginning a new generation. This gesture brought a cohesion and continuity to life from one generation to the next.

In a real sense, we act out the patterns of our parents whether we like it or not. They were our role models when we were young and impressionable. Some of what we learn is useful and some of it is not. We either move beyond our parents by setting a different pattern or we can continue to act out the patterns of our parents. In the end we become explorers, mapping out territory that up to now has been left in the large confine of the "unknown."

> From the primordial womb
> Came the first elements of the divine
> From the Earth
> Came the structure to give it body
> From the Air
> Came the breath to give it life
> From the Fire
> Came the desire to make it more
> From the water
> Came the flow of everlasting life
> A part of the seasons
> Spring, summer, autumn, and winter
> Together they are One

A part of the Goddess.

I am the past
I am my memories
I am the future
I am my dreams
I am who I am now
I am myself
Blessed by the Goddess
By the Lady, blessed be!

The Abundance of Peace and Harmony

Often it is abundance that brings you peace from the outside world. To this end, Fengi and Mengi, two magical giants in the time of the heroic Scandinavian King Frodi, worked a mill whose grindstone magically produced peace and prosperity throughout the land. Unfortunately, the king insisted that they work constantly, only letting them rest for as long as it took them to sing a song.

When the two female giants became angry and exhausted, they sang a magical charm that brought about the king's death. The new king, Mysing, again set Fengi and Mengi to work, only this time grinding salt. They worked so hard and ground so much salt that it overflowed into the sea, making the water forever salty.

Abundance can be an intricate part of peace and harmony, but not when a person works so hard that it brings anger and exhaustion into her life. Life is to be enjoyed, and work and play

need to be balanced together for there to be peace and harmony. It's essential to stop and smell the flowers along the way.

> *Today and everyday, I feel the stress of life being*
> *lifted from my back. Like a weight suddenly gone,*
> *I am energized and feel light as a feather, floating*
> *on the breeze. I work, I play, and I have time for*
> *both, for both are equally important to me.*

> *Goddess,*
> *I ask*
> *When I am truly in need,*
> *Goddess,*
> *Spin your wheel*
> *Bless me with everlasting peace and prosperity.*

I have adapted the following blessing from an ancient verse
written anonymously for the Goddess. It shows that sometimes blessings can be light and humorous. Laughing can
relieve stress and worry. Humor is one of the best defenses
against negativity, the archenemy of peace and harmony.

> *Oh dog, my dog, so dear to me*
> *We're out of luck I plainly see*
> *No truffles have we found today*
> *So let's go to the Goddess and pray*
> *For if her favor we implore*
> *She'll grant us truffles at every door*
> *Then fortune will smile forevermore.*

Derived from Turan, who was originally an Etruscan Goddess, Turanna is known as the "Good Fairy" of peace and love in modern Italy. She is said to be very beautiful and does good things for those who call upon her blessings. Turanna performs her miracles and brings good fortune by means of three winning cards, which in this case represent the dice of ancient mythology. Among the Romans, the highest cast of three dice, three sixes, was called the "Venus-throw," alluding to the association between Turanna and Venus, Roman Goddess of love.

Used extensively by the counterculture during the 1960s, this idea of putting peace and love together as one basic concept is essentially a harmonious one. In the form of the Goddess Turanna, peace and love are fused together with the concept of miracles and good fortune as expressed in the following traditional verse.

Turanna, Turanna!
By the good which thou hast done!
Thou hast ever been so good and generous,
Thou are good as thou art fair,
For of beauty thou art the star!

Oh Good Fairy,
Giver of miracles,
I seek your blessings
Bring magic into my life
Oh Good Fairy,
Giver of Peace and Love,
I seek your blessings
Bring harmony into my life.

Bringing about a More Peaceful Time

The Horae, also known as the "hours" or "seasons," was a group of Greek Goddesses representing the divine aspects of the natural order of the seasons. One of them, Dice, was said to have become so tired of the constant conflicts of humankind that she went to the mountains to wait for a more peaceful time. She finally ascended to the heavens to become the constellation Virgo.

> *Oh Mother of Peace,*
> *Let your divine light spread throughout the world*
> *So all might put down their weapons*
> *And the world can live as One*
> *Now and forevermore*
> *So be it! Blessed be!*

Besides being the hours and seasons, the Horae had the task of ordering and adorning life. At the time when Aphrodite was born from the sea, the Horae welcomed her with tidings of joy. Clothing her with heavenly garments, they put a crown of gold on her head, and then adorned her with golden necklaces and jewels.

The Horae are also the wardens of Olympus and the sky. They open and close the cloudy Gates of Heaven, thus controlling who comes in and out of the realm of the divine. To have their blessings is to be in harmony with the hours, seasons, and natural order of life. To be without their blessings is chaos. You can use blessings to bring divine order and continuity into your life.

Oh Goddess, let me flow with the natural order of life
Bless me with peace of mind
Help me be in harmony with everything in my world
So be it!

Irene is one of the Horae. Her name means "peaceful," and naturally, she is the Greek Goddess of peace. She is depicted as a young woman with a cornucopia, scepter, and torch. The most famous marble statue of Irene was sculpted by Cephisodotus in 380 B.C. The following is a passage written for the Goddess of peace by Ovid Fasti, a Roman poet and writer.

Come peace, your flowing tresses wreathed with
laurel. Let your gentle presence triumph in the
whole world. Let there be no foes. Add incense to
the flames that burn on the altar of peace. Pour a
wine libation. Pray to the deities that peace may
last forever.

As we move further into the twenty-first century, it is becoming essential that we learn to live together peacefully and in harmony. Human history has been one of conflict, both between countries and individuals. If we all visualize world peace, we are one step closer to making it happen. What once was a vision can someday become a reality. We can envision, create, and experience an extraordinary future for humankind. When we all work together, we can learn to live as One.

The following affirming words can be used to create a more peaceful future for our children and all of us.

Goddess of Peace,
I hear you calling to me
I feel your gentle touch
I know you are everywhere
Inside and outside of me
Let there be no boundaries
Between me and you
By the Goddess, blessed be!

With the helping hand of the Goddess
I embrace harmony
With the helping spirit of the Goddess
I embrace serenity
With the helping heart of the Goddess
I embrace understanding.

Today and every day, I see myself becoming more at
peace with myself and with the world around me. I
resolve to end any conflicts that have separated me
from my true self, my family, and my friends.

The Mother of Peace

Mother Mary embodies the Goddess religion as it survives in Christianity. The idea of the "Mother" as the creatrix became obscured in some of the early Christian teachings. So Mother Mary came into being, even though the birth of Christ was later ascribed to immaculate conception, which tries to rob sexuality from women and men. This sexual element is widely recognized in mystery traditions, but later Christians portrayed the sexual union of female and male as somehow negative. The beauty and uniqueness of our whole creation suffers as a result, making us "bad people" needing salvation for our supposed sins.

As spirituality became more paternal, the Goddess movement sought refuge in a few fragmented images that embodied what had come before. As with Kuan Yin, Mother Mary represents the ancient archetype of the Goddess. This archetype has existed since people began to realize that their sustenance and existence came from the generous and divine Mother.

Mary, Mary, Mary,
You who are so good and wise,
And so learned and talented,
Mary, Mary, Mary,
You who are so good and loving
Throughout this world you are known
And revered by all,
Mary, Mary, Mary,
The Mother of us all is always generous,
Granting us fortune and talent.
Mary, Mary, Mary,
I pray to thee, to grant me
Peace and harmony.
By the Lady, blessed be!

I feel a peaceful cloud envelop me
And my spirit soars high within the divine
I feel a harmony that sounds like a symphony
That leads me down the many roads to Oneness.

☾

~ CHAPTER NINE ~

Affirmations, Prayers, and Blessings for Greater Spiritual Awareness

*T*he Goddess is one of the earliest symbols of divinity. It is from her womb that all life comes. It is from her breasts that life is nourished. It is from her fire that life is continually renewed.

Each Mother Goddess has many names and faces, but ultimately these names and faces are all aspects of one multidimensional Goddess. Every Goddess has a light, neutral, and a dark side, and each side has three main aspects, which signify the trinity of the Goddess and the ninefold One. From this trinity, there are many secondary aspects that were developed through time, often by introducing deities from other traditions.

The concept of the one multidimensional Goddess is universal in terms of the human condition. To see life through the eyes of the Goddess is to perceive the divine possibilities in everything. When you flow with the natural harmony of this world, you unlock doors to better health and harmony. You attain greater spiritual awareness that can eventually lead to enlightenment.

Goddess, be in my eyes and how I see things
Goddess, be in my ears and how I hear things
Goddess, be in my spirit and how I perceive things
So that I will always be a part of the whole of divinity
By the grace of the Goddess, blessed be!

Greater spiritual awareness is only reached when we finally attain the divine state of being that we set for ourselves at the dawn of humanity. Expect it, and you will have envisioned what it will be. Desire it, and you will have seen it your mind. Merge with it, and it becomes part of the divine reality, all with the blessing of the Goddess.

The divine is a reflection of ourselves, and we are a reflection of the divine. The power to transform our lives at will is something ascribed to the divine, but it is actually well within the bounds of human achievement. We can all become divine extensions of the overall power of the Goddess.

Today, I know the Goddess lives within me! She
grants me her knowledge and love of all things.

Goddess of wisdom,
I ask you with all of my being
Please grant me your divine gifts
Forever guide me
By the Goddess, blessed be!

The Goddess is my light with each new day
The Goddess feeds my soul in every way,
She walks beside me, always there to guide me
She is there with me, come what may.

Moon Goddess of the mysteries,
Queen of the waves, tides, and sea,
Beloved lady, shine your silver light
I call you bright star of the night
Beloved Mother of the womb and well,
Next to your beauty, all others pale
I call upon your laughter and love
Beloved wise woman, spinner of life
Weaver of dreams, and sacred wife
Fair Goddess of wisdom, I call thee
Moon Goddess of beauty, come to me!
May I be One with your divine light
May I feel you with me day and night
By the grace of the Goddess, so be it!

How Things Began

In the beginning only formless chaos existed in a shapeless primordial soup. As chaos began to settle and take form, this form became Gaea, the Earth, who existed before time began. Time later became one of her offspring. In the timeless expanse before creation, she was all that existed.

Longing for love, Gaea created a son, Uranus, the heaven. The mating of heaven and Earth released Gaea's creative force, which then produced other offspring. Because of Uranus's jealousy, Gaea hid them from him. Eventually, her son Cronos killed Uranus, and in the ensuing rain that fell on the Earth Mother Gaea, the "Erinyes," giants, ash tree nymphs, and the "Meliae," who are our human ancestors, sprang to life.

Thank you, Goddess, for the life you give to me. It is from your divine spirit that I was born and continue to live. I ask for your blessings so that my family and I will always be healthy, wealthy, happy, and wise.

May I always be in tune with the Goddess and she with me, so that I always take time to watch the beauty of butterflies no matter how busy I feel.

Today and every day, I let the light of the Goddess into my life. I stop to take a deep breath and feel the love that she brings with her. It is a love that lights my soul on fire, and I know I have finally come home.

My Goddess,
You are all things to me;
You are nothingness
You are everything
You are the trees in the fall
You are the flowers in the spring
You are the food I eat
You are the air I breathe
You are the water I drink
You are the Earth I walk upon
You are the thoughts I think
You are the feelings I feel
You are the dreams I dream

I am you, and you are me
We are One. Blessed be!

Gaea was also the primeval prophet who inspired the oracles at
Delphi, Dodona, and elsewhere. Delphi was considered the
Earth's Navel. Because Gaea came into being before the existence of time, she is impervious to the linear boundaries of
time. Past, present, and future are one circular flow. In terms of
divination, the future can be perceived by accessing this circular flow of time, particularly with the blessings of the Goddess.

Great Goddess, I pray you
Help me feel a boundless love for all the world
In all its height and depth and broad extent
Love unrestrained, without hate or fear
Thank you, Lady, for living here on Earth is life divine.
May every creature abound in well-being, love, and
   peace.

Today and every day, I am the peace, calm, and
harmony of the Mother Earth's lush green
valleys. I am the flow of her clear, rushing rivers
and streams. I am the wisdom of her trees
standing firm. I am the strength of her stones. I
am her snowcapped peaks of spirit. I am the
mystery of the unknown yet to be discovered and
born. I am, indeed, a child of the Goddess.

The Lady is the light
The light of my eyes

The Lady is the Light
The light of my heart
The Lady is the light
The light of my soul
The Lady is the light
The Lady is the flame.

The Goddess Figures in Tarot

Divination systems tap into that part of the Goddess that is circular and timeless. Like a giant computer database, the future is within your reach as long as you know how to access it. Calling on these many divinations utilizes the energy of the Goddess, making divining more powerful.

Divination is a way of communicating with the divine. When you use divination, it's like holding a mirror up to yourself and tapping into your divine nature. In this way, divination tools such as Tarot cards are not only fortune-telling tools but also a form of do-it-yourself therapy. It becomes a way to unlock the secrets inside of yourself, helping you to move in a more positive direction and attain your personal goals.

In the case of Tarot, some of the cards in the major arcana relate specifically to the energy of the Goddess. The following Goddess cards and corresponding affirmations can be used to access the power of the Goddess within the archetypes of the Tarot.

☾ The High Priestess is a card of intuition, clarity, knowledge, and independence.

*I trust and honor my intuition. I value my sense
of integrity. I am a directed and aware person.*

(The Empress is a card of nurturing, care, support, elegance,
and beauty.

*I am a supportive and nurturing person. I enjoy
beauty, elegance, and harmony. I give wisely and
receive wisely.*

(Strength is a card of power, courage, vitality, passion, lust,
and fortitude.

*I enjoy expressing my enthusiasm, energy,
humor, and vitality in all that I experience. I am
a person of strength and courage.*

(The Moon is a card of truth, romance, love, and choice. It is
a magic mirror.

*I enjoy what is mysterious in myself and others. I
enjoy making positive choices. I value honesty,
truth, and integrity.*

(The Star is a card of hope, confidence, vision, recognition,
and guidance.

*I have a vision of the future that is both hopeful
and confident. I recognize my need for divine
guidance, and know that in the future it will give
me greater spiritual awareness.*

A Manifestation of Time

A manifestation of Kali, the queen of time, is Tara. She is the Hindu star Goddess, who as a star in the night sky is beautiful and self-perpetuating. She is the hunger that drives all life. Along with this initial hunger came other hungers, such as the spiritual hunger that longs to be released from the boundaries of the physical world, and move in spirit form into the whole of the divine.

> *Divine Mother, let your vitality empower my*
> *body. Let your wisdom empower my mind, and*
> *let your infinite spirit empower my spiritual*
> *awareness.*
>
> *Today, I take charge of my physical hungers and*
> *addictions, releasing them, and putting in their*
> *place a hunger to know who I am spiritually and*
> *to be at One with the Goddess.*
>
> *Expect, and it will be given to you*
> *Look, and you will see a door open to you*
> *Desire, and it will become real to you*
> *Merge, and you feel the energy of Goddess.*

Because of Tara's connection to spiritual hunger, she is Goddess of self-mastery and mysticism, who sometimes appears as the person who ferries people through the world of delusion to the world of knowledge. In one of her aspects as the White Tara of meditation, she stares at a person through three eyes to remind him that if he looks beyond the fear of death and the unknown, she will be there waiting to enlighten him.

> *I am a star of light. I value who I am. My thoughts and actions positively benefit myself and others.*

> *Tonight and every night, I pray to the Great Lady that I may find comfort in knowing my life will unfold naturally. I allow myself to flow into the eternity of my true nature, which is unfathomable, unconquerable, and boundless. No longer bound by limitations, I am free and One with the divine*

> *I am the Goddess*
> *And the Goddess is me*
> *Every morning when I awake*
> *It is her image that I take.*
> *I am the Goddess*
> *And the Goddess is me*
> *Every evening when I sleep*
> *It is her dream that I keep.*
> *I am the Goddess*
> *And the Goddess is me*
> *Blessed be!*

From the One Came the Many

In Egyptian creation mythology, at first only Atum existed. Both female and male, Atum was complete, whole, and perfect. Mass without form, she was both everything and nothing at the same time.

She wished for companionship to experience her own divinity, so through the union of self with self, Atum created two offspring: a son, Shu, who is yesterday, and a daughter, Telnut, who is tomorrow. They have two children: Nut, a daughter, who is heaven, and Geis, a son, who is Earth. The subsequent love of heaven and Earth bore a thousand souls, who then began to populate heaven and Earth. Their children became both the deities and mortals.

I see sunshine
Let the Goddess of Light shine,
Her rays soothe my soul
And I realize everything is mine,
I am an aspect of the Goddess,
I am who I am;
I am every aspect of the Goddess
I am she and she is me.

Goddess of Earth,
Bless me with worldly abundance
Goddess of Heaven,
Bless me with spiritual abundance
By the grace of the Goddess, so be it!

Today and every day, I feel my connection to the
divine becoming stronger. I am humble, I am
divine, I am the balance in between.

From the Nameless

From the unmanifested, that place where nothing has form or name, came the Celtic Goddess Kerridwen. Originally she was the sun and moon and only later came to be associated solely with the moon. She is the universal Goddess in Celtic and Welsh mystery traditions; all the other Goddesses are aspects of Kerridwen. Like her Greek and Egyptian counterparts, she is the unmanifested before it becomes manifested into form.

Once things attain form, they become named because of the human need to name everything that has form and to ignore everything that doesn't. We are all created from Oneness, which has no form or name in the unmanifested, and which takes on all different forms and names in the manifested.

The Goddess is the conduit between human perception and the divine, essentially from the micro to the macro view of life.

Wondrous Mother,
The cells of my body are made of light,
My mind is made of you
For you are spirit and I am spirit
That which is eternal.

*In this reality and every reality, I work toward
increasing my spiritual awareness. Every morning
when I awake, I step into a new perception that is
both forgiving and positive. Every night when I go
to sleep, I give myself the suggestion that I am
living the life I want to live, and I am improving
upon it on a daily basis.*

Prayer Stones

A technique of the early Celts, putting the energy of spiritual
awareness into a stone is something that has been practiced for
thousands of years. Whether an amulet or talisman, your affirmations, prayers, and blessings can be programmed into a
stone. You can use the stone to empower your life patterns.

Begin by picking a stone that you feel a kinship with. To
clear it of any energetic charge it might have, hold it in your
power hand. In your mind's eye, imagine a clear mountain
stream washing the stone clean. Hold the thought in your
mind, and pulse a breath of air through your nose while seeing
the stone clean of energy.

Now, take a moment and imagine what sort of energy you
want to put in your prayer stone. Suggestions include that of a
Goddess or particular aspect of a Goddess with whom you
have a rapport. You could also program your stone with a feeling of greater spiritual awareness or a suggestion that each day
be a divine experience.

Once you decide what you want to put in your prayer
stone, put the stone in the palm of your power hand and close

your fingers around it. Clearly and specifically imagine what you want programmed in your stone, and say,

> *Stone of prayer,*
> *I fill you with my thoughts*
> *By my will and desire*
> *And the grace of the Goddess*
> *You now flow with the energy of my prayer*
> *By the Lady, so be it!*

Pulse a breath of air through your nose while holding the image of your prayer in your mind. Imagine a thread of light moving from your mind into the stone, filling it full of your prayer until your stone resonates with a power of its own. You now have a prayer stone that you can use to tap into the Goddess and become more spiritually aware. Keep your stone on your person, in your purse, or on your altar to empower your prayer.

Feminine Empowerment

The Roman Mother Goddess Juno rules over the entire reproductive cycle of women. As such, she embodies the essence of femininity. Within the Roman concept, each man has a "genius," the spirit that made him alive and sexually active, and every woman her "juno," an enlivening inner force of femaleness.

> *I am Goddess,*
> *Hear me scream*

The Earth is in trouble,
She needs our help now
May we tune our spirits toward saving the Mother
May we heal and protect her always
By the grace of the Goddess, so be it!

Today and every day I am proud to be a woman,
created in the image of the Goddess. I respect who
I am and give divine thanks every day I am alive
and well. May the Goddess always give me her
blessings, and may the future always be bright.

Juno is also the Goddess of time. Again, this shows that the Mother Goddess exists beyond the bounds of the normal perceptions of time. Within this timeless void, information about the past, present, and future can be readily accessed, depending upon your intention and expectation.

Goddess of time,
I ask for your blessings
Let me age gracefully
And always be full of your vitality
And eternal spirit.

Today, I work toward moving my mind beyond
the normal bounds of time. No longer will I think
in terms of yesterday, today, and tomorrow. I now
see time and life as being circular.

Some nights, I stay up till dawn,
As the moon sometimes does for the sun,

Be a full bucket pulled up the dark way
Of a well, then lifted out into light.
The Goddess opens my wings
The Goddess makes boredom and hurt disappear,
The Goddess fills the cup in front of us
I taste only divinity.

(Adapted from a verse by Rumi)

The Many Faces of the Goddess

As mentioned earlier, the many faces of Goddess are apparent wherever you go. Life is created by female energy; to think otherwise is to struggle with the natural flow of the universe. Women produce offspring, not men.

I recently read an account on the Internet about a woman who had an interesting and profound relationship with butterflies. Her two-year-old son fell into a pool, and it was a butterfly that woke her up and made her aware of the impending disaster.

At the same time that the butterfly story was on the Internet, the news carried accounts of several fathers, including a technician and high school teacher, and a few mothers, who were so out of touch with things that they forgot their young children in the back seat of their cars. As it was summertime, the infants all died from the heat.

In one case, a woman was very in tune with nature and her child. She was given a gift by the Goddess, the butterfly spirit, that helped her to save her child. In the other cases, the

parents were tragically out of touch with themselves, their children, the power of nature, and the Goddess. Our deepest
prayers go out to them and those that have passed on.

We all need to stay in touch with nature in the form of the
Goddess, and we need to stay in touch with our children and
ourselves. We need to take time from our hurried lives, to slow
down and really embrace and live life, not just get through the
day. Both women and men can benefit from the love, guidance, and protection of the Great Goddess, for we all have the
divine feminine within.

> *I am surrounded by love.*
> *I give thanks for all the good things in my life.*
> *I ask the Goddess to help me be aware and alert*
> *I ask the Goddess to help me let go of pain and fear*
> *I ask the Goddess to help me feel love.*
>
> *Dear Goddess, please grant me the serenity*
> *To meet each new day even when things seem*
>   *unbearable.*
> *Dear Goddess, give me the strength*
> *To reach new heights day after day*
> *Even when things seem unattainable.*
> *By the grace of the Goddess, so be it!*
>
> *Today and every day, I become more aware of the*
> *connections between myself and the people*
> *around me, particularly with my immediate*
> *family. I understand my children as divine*

children, and myself as a human being with
divine potential. Every day I become more and
more aware of our divinity.

Hail to the lady of the stars
Hail to the lady of the sky
Hail to the lady of the Earth
She who is life, death, and rebirth
I give my thanks to her continued blessings
In perfect love and perfect peace
She is always with me
In body, mind, and spirit
She is my eternal light
Guiding me through the valley of darkness
Into the mountains of the sun,
Help me to forgive myself and others
Blessed be the Goddess
Blessed be the One
From humble beginnings
I aspire to be divine.
By the grace of the Goddess
Blessed be!

Asking the Goddess for a Boon

Boons are divine gifts from the Lady. In the evening after dark, begin by lighting a candle. Merge with the flame, and say something like,

Moon Goddess, Queen of the night,
In all of your splendor bright,
Send down your silvery beams,
And open the door of dreams.
Moon Goddess, Queen of lunar power,
Come to me at this enchanted hour.

Then say,

I am (state your name).
Great One, I pray that you will grant me a boon.

Next, think about the good things you have done in the past. Merge with the candle again, and say,

I have done these good works in the past.
(State your good works aloud to the Goddess.)
You have seen my honest effort.
Please, Great One, grant me this boon
So I might create my deepest dreams.
Praise to you. Blessed be, Great One!
Blessed be! Blessed be! Blessed be!

Continue gazing at the candlelight, and merge with your creative source. If you prefer, you can imagine going deep into a magical well, and pulling up ideas and creative thoughts. Do this for at least fifteen minutes.

May the eternal Goddess always bless you, and her divine love surround you. May the inner light of your spirit always guide you on your life path.

☾

Goddesses Around the World

Aife or Aoife (Celtic): Consort of the sea god, Manannan.

Ailinn (Celtic): Goddess of affection, romance, and love.

Aine (Celtic): Goddess of Earth and Sun, queen of the Faery, mate to Lugh.

Airmed (Celtic): Goddess of witchcraft and herb lore.

Akupera (Hindu): Goddess of moonlight.

Anadyomene (Greek): Sea-born Goddess of sexuality.

Andraste or Andrasta (Celtic): Goddess of fertility, warriors, and victory.

Anahita (Persian): "Golden Mother," who is healer, mother, and protector.

Anna Perenna (Roman): Goddess of sexuality and fertility.

Annapurna (Hindu): Great Mother Goddess of abundance. Giver of plenty.

Anu, Danu (Celtic): Mother Goddess of knowledge, healing, and fertility.

Anuket or Anukis (Egyptian): Goddess of the river and fertility.

Aphrodite (Greek): Goddess of love, pleasure, and beauty.

Ardwinna (Celtic): Goddess of the forests and woods.

Arianrhod (Celtic): Stellar and lunar Goddess, her palace is the Corona Borealis, known as Caer Arianrhod (The Northern Crown).

Artemis (Greek): Goddess of fruitful abundance and twin sister of Apollo.

Artio (Celtic): Goddess of fertility and wildlife, portrayed as a bear.

Astarte (Phoenician): Great Mother Goddess, associated with
the planet Venus. Later assimilated into the Assyro-
Babylonian Culture.

Athena (Greek): Goddess of wisdom and warriors in battle.

Atum (Egyptian): Both female and male, she is complete, whole,
and perfect. Mass without form, she is both everything and
nothing at the same time.

Badb or Badhbh, Badb Catha, Bav, Bov, Bodhbh (Celtic):
Druidess of the Tuatha De Danann and Goddess of war,
inspiration, fury, and wisdom.

Banba (Celtic): Goddess of the sacred land.

Bast, Bastet (Egyptian): Cat Goddess of fertility, pleasure, dancing, music, and love.

Belisama (Celtic): Young Goddess of fire whose name means
"like unto flame" and "the bright and shining one." Wife of
Belenus.

Belisana (Celtic): Goddess of healing, laughter, and the forests.
Associated with the sun's warmth and woodland plants and
animals.

Blathnat (Celtic): "Little Flower," Goddess of sex.

Blodenwedd (Blodewedd, Blodeuedd) (Celtic): Beautiful and
treacherous sun and moon Goddess, associated with the
white owl, dawn, primroses, broom, cockle, oak, and
meadowsweet.

Bo Find (Celtic): Goddess of fertility.

Boann or Boi, Boanna (Celtic): Mother of the herds, Goddess of
fertility, inspiration, and the river Boyne, wife of the Dagda.

Branwen (Welsh): Goddess of love, called the White-Bosomed
One and Venus of the Northern Sea. Her name means White
Raven.

Bridget, Brighid, Brede (Celtic): Fertility Goddess of the Sacred
Fire, the sun, hearth, and home. The bride Goddess of inspiration, poetry, medicine, healing, and smithcraft.

Caer (Celtic): Swan maiden, wife of Angus.

Cailleach (Pre-Celtic): Goddess of earth, sky, moon, and sun,
who controlled the seasons and weather.

Calliope (Greek): Muse of epic poetry.

Cherubim (Hebrew): Goddess/God of sexuality and inter-
course.

Cilleac Bheur (Celtic): Goddess of winter, whose staff can freeze
the ground and wither the crops.

Clio (Greek): Muse of history.

Cliodna (Celtic): Bird Goddess and Faerie Queen associated
with extraordinary beauty, shape-shifting, apples, accompa-
nied by three magical birds.

Coventina (Celtic): Goddess of the well and the womb of the
Earth, associated with healing springs, sacred wells, childbirth, renewal, and the Earth.

Dana or Danu, Dannu, Anu, Ana, Anna, Ann, Don (Celtic): The
Mother Goddess from whom Tuatha De Danann were
descended. Goddess of nature, wisdom, and creation.

Deirdre (Celtic): "One who gives warning," or the older form
Derdriu, "Oak prophet." A humanized Goddess in the Red
Branch tale of the Exile of the sons of Uisnach. The daughter
of the God Morgan.

Demeter (Greek): Goddess of fertility, marriage, and prosperity.

Devi (Hindu): The Goddess whose energy continues to protect
the world from chaos.

Dia Griene (Celtic): The daughter of the sun.

Diana (Roman): Goddess of moonlight and the hunt.

Edain or Etain (Celtic): Goddess of beauty, grace, and wife of King Mider, one of the "White Ladies" of the Faery.

Elayne or Elen, Elen Lwyddawg (Celtic): Powerful Goddess of leadership and war.

Eostre or Ostara (Celtic): Goddess of Spring and fertility.

Epona (Celtic): Goddess of fertility, power, and abundance.

Erato (Greek): Muse of love poetry, mimicry, and pantomime.

Eri of the Golden Hair (Celtic): Goddess of love and sexuality.

Erie (Eriu) (Celtic): The triple mother Goddess of Erin, sometimes known as Ir, from which the land of Ir in Ireland is derived. Shape-shifter and Goddess of Sovereignty of the Land.

Eurynome (Greek): The mother of all pleasure, whose embodiment is the beautiful triplets, the Graces; splendor, abundance, joyousness.

Euterpe (Greek): Muse of music and lyric poetry.

Ezili (Haitian): Goddess generous to the point of extravagance with her followers, from whom she expects the same in return.

Fand (Celtic): Shape-shifter and Faery Queen of Ireland, associated with the sea gull.

Fengi and Mengi (Norse): Two magical giants who, in the time of the heroic Scandinavian King Frodi, worked a mill whose grindstone magically produced peace and prosperity.

Findabair (Celtic): Goddess of Connacht and the Otherworld, of beauty, grace, and love.

Fliodhas (Celtic): Goddess of the woodlands, protector of animals and forests, associated with the doe.

Flora (Roman): Goddess of fertility, sex, promiscuity, and Spring.

Fortuna (Roman): Lady Luck, Goddess of love and sexuality.

Freya (Norse): Goddess of Love, beauty, passion, and fertility.

Frigga (Norse): Goddess of feminine arts, associated with hawks and falcons.

Gaea (Greek): The Goddess who embodies the Earth and has existed before time began.

Graces (Roman, Greeks called them the Charites): Three Goddesses embodying grace of manner. They are Thaleia (abundance), Aglaia (splendor and radiance), and Eurphrosyne (joy and happiness).

Grainne (Celtic): Young maiden who becomes a Goddess of love.

Harmonia (Greek): Goddess of music, dance, and poetry.

Hathor (Egyptian): Goddess of love, Mother of creation, and mistress of everything beautiful.

Heket (Egyptian): Frog Goddess of childbirth and creation.

Helen (Greek): Moon Goddess of childbirth, love, and fertility.

Hera (Greek): Goddess of women and their sexuality, including matrimony.

Hertha (Celtic): Goddess of fertility, Spring, the Earth, rebirth, and healing.

Hestia (Greek): She is the fire of the hearth, living in the center of every home.

Horae (Greek): A group of Greek Goddesses representing the divine aspects of the natural order of the seasons.

Inanna (Sumerian): Mother Goddess who brought civilization to humankind.

Irene (Greek): Goddess of peace.

Ishtar (Babylonian): Goddess of love, beauty, and war, associated with Venus, the morning star.

Isis (Egyptian): Mother Goddess, embodiment of femininity.

Isong (African): Goddess of fertility.

Juno (Roman): Mother Goddess who rules over the entire reproductive cycle of women.

Kerridwen or Cerridwyn, Ceridwyn (Celtic): Goddess of knowledge and wisdom who possesses the cauldron of inspiration.

Kuan Yin (Chinese): Goddess of compassion and beauty.

Lakshmi (Hindu): Goddess of beauty and good fortune.

Letha (Celtic): Midsummer harvest Goddess.

Maat (Egyptian): Goddess of truth and balance.

Macha or Emhain Macha (Celtic): Threefold sun Goddess of
fertility, war, and ritual games, associated with the horse,
raven, and crow.

Maya (Hindu): Goddess of creativity.

Medb or Maeve, Mab, Medhbh (Celtic): Warrior Queen and
Goddess of sex, fertility, and sovereignty.

Meditrina (Roman): The Roman Goddess of medicine, wine,
and health.

Mei or Mai, Meia (Celtic): Mother of Gwalchmei and a solar and
Earth Goddess.

Melpomene (Greek): Muse of tragedies and songs of mourning.

Meskhenet (Egyptian): Goddess of childbirth.

Modrona or Modron, Madrona, Matrona (Celtic): The Great
Mother of Mabon (light).

Mokosh (Slavic): The great Goddess of the Earth.

Morgan Le Fey (Celtic): Faerie Queen, sorceress, shape-shifter,
and beautiful enchantress.

Morgana (Celtic): The Death Mother, Goddess of war and fertility.

Morrigan or Morrigana (Celtic): "The Phantom Queen or Great

Queen," and a sea Goddess, she is the triple Goddess of War, who shape-shifts into a raven.

Morrigu (Celtic): Dark Gray Lady and Queen of the Sea, Goddess of life, death, and magic.

Muses (Greek): Originally three Goddesses who later became nine. They oversaw and inspired poetry, music, and the other creative arts.

Mother Mary (Christian): Christian archetype of the Mother Goddess. She gives birth to the son of the divine.

Nantosuelta (Celtic): River Goddess.

Nemetona (Celtic): Protectress of the sacred Drynemeton; Warrior Goddess of the oak groves and patroness of thermal springs.

Nephthys (Egyptian): Goddess of dreams, divination, and hidden knowledge.

Niamh or Neeve of the Golden Hair (Celtic): Goddess of love and beauty.

Nimue or Niniane, Niviene, Nymenche (Celtic): Student and teacher to Merlin, her consort.

Norns (Norse): Three sisters, who control the destiny of everyone. Urd creates patterns, Verdandi weaves them and gives them structure, and Sculd unravels them, throwing them back into the unmanifested.

Omamama (Native American): The Cree ancestral Goddess of beauty, fertility, gentleness, and love.

Oshun (African): Goddess of love, pleasure, beauty, and dancing.

Parvati (Hindu): Goddess of marital blessing.

Penelope (Greek): Spring Goddess of fertility and sexuality.

Pi-Hsai Yuan-Chin (Chinese): Goddess of childbirth who

brings health and good fortune to the newborn and protection to the mother.

Polyhymnia (Greek): Muse of hymns, mimic art, and harmony.

Psyche (Greek): Goddess of love.

Rhiannon (Celtic): Queen Mother, Queen Mare, or the Great Queen.

Rosemerta (Celtic): Goddess of fertility, beauty, and love.

Sadv (Celtic): Ancient deer Goddess of the forests and nature.

Saga (Norse): Goddess of poetry and daughter of Odin, said to be an aspect or face of the Mother Goddess Frigga.

Selene (Greek/Roman): Moon and love Goddess.

Shakti (Hindu): Great Mother Goddess, who embodies feminine energy.

Sheila na Gig (Celtic): Goddess of sex, birth, passion, and laughter.

Sirona (Celtic): Solar and astral Goddess.

Sulis (Celtic): Goddess of healing and warm springs.

Taillte (Celtic): Earth Goddess and foster mother to Lugh.

Tara (Hindu): Star Goddess, she is the hunger that drives all life.

Terpsichore (Greek): Muse of dancing and music, in particular the choral song.

Thalia (Greek): The festive Muse of comedy and idyllic poetry.

Tiamat (Mesopotamian): Great Mother Goddess, who took the form of a dragon.

Tlazolteotl (Peruvian): Goddess of love.

Triana (Celtic): The Triple Goddess: Sun-Ana, Earth-Ana, and Moon-Ana, also of healing, knowledge, higher love, and wisdom.

Turanna, Turan (originally Etruscan, later Italian): Known as the "Good Fairy" of peace and love.

Urania (Greek): Muse of astronomy and cosmological poetry.

Var (Scandinavian): Love Goddess.

Venus (Roman): Goddess of love and sexuality.

Vesta (Roman): Goddess of fire and the hearth.

Viviana or Vivian, Vivien (Celtic): Goddess of love, birth, life, mothers, childbirth, and children. Her consort is Merlin.

Voluptas (Roman): Goddess of pleasure and sensuality.

Voluspa (Norse): Goddess known as a famous seer.

Bibliography

Arrien, Angeles. *The Tarot Handbook*. Sonoma, CA: Arcus Publishing Co., 1987.

Bernstein, Frances, Ph.D. *Classical Living*. San Francisco: HarperSanFrancisco, 2000.

Blair, Nancy. *Amulets of the Goddess*. Oakland, CA: Wingbow Press, 1993.

Bolen, Jean Shinoda, M.D. *Goddesses in Everywoman*. San Francisco: Harper & Row, Publishers, 1984.

Bonwick, James. *Irish Druids and Old Irish Religions*. New York: Dorset, 1986.

Bulfinch, Thomas. *Bulfinch's Mythology*. Garden City, NY: Garden City Publishing Co., Inc., 1938.

Cameron, Julia. *Heart Steps*. New York: Jeremy P Tarcher/Putnam, 1997.

Campbell, Joseph. *The Power of Myth*. New York: Doubleday, 1988.

Canfield, Jack, Mark Victor Hansen, and Les Hewitt. *The Power of Focus*. Deerfield Beach, FL: Health Communications, Inc., 2000.

Dossey, Larry. *Healing Words*. San Francisco: HarperSanFrancisco, 1997.

Ford, Patrick K., trans. *The Mabinogi and Other Medieval Welsh Tales*. Berkeley and Los Angeles: University of California Press, 1977.

Gimbutas, Marija. *The Goddesses and Gods of Old Europe*. Berkeley and Los Angeles: University of California Press, 1982.

Gimbutas, Marija. *The Language of the Goddess*. San Francisco: Harper & Row, 1989.

Green, Miranda J. *Dictionary of Celtic Myth and Legend.* New York: Thames and Hudson, 1997.

Harner, Michael. *The Way of the Shaman.* New York: Bantam, 1986.

Henderson, Helene and Sue Ellen Thompson, eds. *Holidays, Festival, and Celebrations of the World Dictionary.* Detroit, MI: Omnigraphics, Inc., 1997.

Houston, Jean. *The Passion of Isis and Osiris.* New York: Random House, 1995.

Jay, Roni. *The Book of Goddesses.* Hauppauge, NY: Barron's, 2000.

Johnson, Cait, and Maura D. Shaw. *Celebrating the Great Mother.* Rochester, VT: Inner Traditions, 1995.

Jung, Carl G. *The Archetypes of the Collective Unconscious.* Princeton, NJ: Princeton University Press, 1990.

Knight, Sirona. *Celtic Traditions.* New York: Citadel Press, 2000.

———. *Dream Magic.* San Francisco: HarperSanFrancisco, 2000.

———. *Exploring Celtic Druidism.* Franklin Lakes, NJ: New Page Books, 2001.

———. *Greenfire: Making Love with the Goddess.* St. Paul, MN: Llewellyn Publications, 1995.

———. *The Little Giant Encyclopedia of Runes.* New York: Sterling Publishing Co., 2000.

———. *Love, Sex, and Magick.* New York: Citadel Press, 1999.

———. *Moonflower: Erotic Dreaming with the Goddess.* St. Paul, MN: Llewellyn Publications, 1996.

———. *The Pocket Guide to Celtic Spirituality.* Freedom, CA: Crossing Press, 1998.

———. *The Pocket Guide to Crystals and Gemstones.* Freedom, CA: Crossing Press, 1998.

———. *The Witch and Wizard Training Guide.* New York: Citadel Press, 2001.

Knight, Sirona, et al. *The Shapeshifter Tarot.* St. Paul, MN: Llewellyn Publications, 1998.

Knight, Sirona, and Patricia Telesco. *The Wiccan Web.* New York: Citadel Press, 2001.

Leach, Maria, ed. *Standard Dictionary of Folklore, Mythology, and Legend.* New York: Funk & Wagnalls Co., 1950.

Linn, Denise. *The Secret Language of Signs.* New York: Ballantine Book, 1996.

Monaghan, Patricia. *The Book of Goddesses and Heroines.* St Paul, MN: Llewellyn Publications, 1990.

Oman, Maggie, ed. *Prayers for Healing.* Berkeley, CA: Conari Press, 1997.

Rector-Page, Linda. *Healthy Healing.* Sonora, CA: Healthy Healing Publications, 1992.

Roberts, Alison. *Hathor Rising.* Rochester, VT: Inner Traditions International, 1995, 1997.

Sheldrake, Rupert. *A New Science of Life.* Rochester, VT: Inner Traditions, 1995.

Squire, Charles. *Celtic Myth and Legend.* Franklin Lakes, NJ: New Page Books, 2001.

Stewart, R. J. *Celtic Gods, Celtic Goddesses.* New York: Sterling Publishing Co., 1990.

Telesco, Patricia. *A Charmed Life.* Franklin Lakes, NJ: New Page Books, 2000.

Teish, Luisa. *Jambalaya.* San Francisco: Harper & Row, 1986.

Walker, Barbara. *The Woman's Encyclopedia of Myths and Secrets.* San Francisco: Harper & Row, 1983.

Wilshire, Donna. *Virgin Mother Crone.* Rochester, VT: Inner Traditions, 1994.

Yeats, W. B., ed. *Fairy & Folk Tales of Ireland.* New York: Macmillan Publishing Co., 1983.